Pro Wrestling

FIELD GUIDE

Kristian Pope

Legend and Lore

©2005 KP Books

Published by

kp books

An Imprint of F+W Publications

700 East State Street • Iola, WI 54990-0001
715-445-2214 • 888-457-2873

Our toll-free number to place an order or obtain
a free catalog is (800) 258-0929.

Materials excerpted from *The Encyclopedia of
Professional Wrestling*, 2nd Edition © 2003 Kristian Pope &
Ray Whebbe Jr., used with permission.

Library of Congress Catalog Number: 2005924815

ISBN: 0-89689-267-0

Designed by Kay Sanders
Edited by Tracy L. Schmidt

Printed in the United States of America

Contents

Contributing photographs by Dr. Mike Lano (wrealano@aol.com)
and The Wrestling Revue Archives (www.wrestlingrevue.com).

Steve Austin is arguably wrestling's most charismatic star of all-time.

Introduction

Heroes, villains, winners, and losers. Pro wrestling has it all. And that's why we love it.

Despite computer graphics, mainstream publicity, pyrotechnic tricks and slick television production, the core of pro wrestling really hasn't changed much over 100 years. And neither have the fans, who retain an insatiable desire for the sport.

From closet fans to impassioned viewers, we all share a love for wrestling. At times, we're fans whose eyes gaze in wonderment at the spectacle. Remember when nearly 60,000 fans jammed the Toronto Sky Dome for Wrestlemania 18 to witness Hulk Hogan versus The Rock? At other times, we're cheerleaders. Who can't be affected by the raw, unbridled charisma of the performers? Sometimes we're critics. We get frustrated with storylines that make no sense, or mad at gimmicks that rub us wrong. It's all part of being a fan.

Little had been published about pro wrestling until a boom in the 1980s. But why? Despite business downtrends, wrestling still embarrasses real sports like Major League Baseball and college athletics in cable television ratings.

It seems more books are written about America's favorite pastime, baseball, in one year's time than have been written about the "Sport of Kings" in 100 years. The media seemed to only take potshots at wrestling. As a result, promoters felt snubbed by the media and press. In turn, they were protective of their business.

The notion of exposing the business, or admitting that pro wrestling had predetermined outcomes, was a mortal sin. Based largely on tradition from wrestling's late 19th-century carnival days, no one was allowed to know about wrestling's facade. Aside from inner-circle wrestlers and promoters, only a chosen few were allowed to be part of the backstage fraternity. That privilege came only after a process of paying dues and a so-called security check that would make the KGB proud.

The word "fake" has caused more than a few involved in wrestling to be upset with the press. In 1985, Hulk Hogan, who was America's most famous wrestling hero, demonstrated a chokehold on actor Richard Belzer that sent him into oblivion. Belzer was knocked out and needed stitches. Some say Hogan played rough because earlier, Belzer called wrestling fake during their interview together.

A year earlier, Hogan's rough, Southern pal, "Dr." D. David Schultz, cracked ABC investigative reporter John Stossel

Farmer Burns often displayed his amazing neck strength by putting himself in a hangman's noose.

Circa Randy Savage proudly displays his WCW world championship belt on his way to the ring.

upside the head. The journalist was left with permanent ear damage for questioning the reality of wrestling. Apparently, being part of the media covering professional wrestling can be a serious hazard to one's well being. That fact, combined with the long-standing book publisher's comical belief that wrestling fans didn't care to read, helps to explain why so few truthful books about pro wrestling have been written. Until now, anyway.

For most of the modern day, fans of wrestling history were shunned by the public for enjoying wrestling. Those who found joy in it were seemingly forced to hide their knowledge and would have to meet other wrestling fanatics in backyards, ball fields, and basements. Every neighborhood had wrestling fans, but its detractors were plenty. Those who stuck together had a common bond. Their demand for more information grew and underground avenues, like fan clubs, provided the best way to get ring gossip.

From 1940 to 1980, when a wrestler succeeded in garnering mainstream coverage, we all shared in the glory. If an Associated Press photo was published in the daily newspaper, we all cheered. When a wrestler was seen on a television show or a film, we all watched. As soon as the mainstream jumped on wrestling's popularity and rode its coattails for profit, we all wondered, "What took them so long?"

At one time, wrestling magazines gave the only look into its wackiness. In the 1950s, youths could only wonder if Mongolians really had big muscles and odd haircuts. They wondered if Sicilians all looked like Tony Altamore and Captain Lou Albano. What kind of match would the then World Wide Wrestling Federation world champion, Bruno Sammartino, have against the National Wrestling Alliance champion Lou Thesz? Prior to videotapes, the only place to gain information about other wrestling leagues was through the newsstand magazines. Playing to promoter's fears about revealing the truth, magazines covered up wrestlers' real names and backgrounds and wrote only what they thought promoters and fans wanted to read. Nobody, so it seemed, was to be let in on the secrets.

By the early 1980s, videotape-trading fans bonded through the mail. All of a sudden, because of video, news traveled a lot faster in the mail than what was found through newsstand magazines. Today, those footprints of trading info are found through sources on the Internet. Prior to 1985, any official information offered about a wrestler was standard drivel and, often times, fabricated. For many fans, the thirst for truth was a driving force in their lives, so they pursued accurate information.

Eventually, fans were let in on the real information. Through newsletters, which boasted regional focuses, fans in

Who can argue that Lou Thesz wasn't the greatest world champion ever?

The Rock gets a hold on the legend, Jerry Lawler.

Tacoma, Wash., could be in tune with what was happening in Tallahassee, Fla. Soon, with an emerging younger generation of wrestlers, editors of the newsletters began to garner access to backstage gossip and news. Newsletters like Dave Meltzer's *Wrestling Observer* and Steve Beverly's *Matwatch*, read like miniature trade magazines. Nowadays, backstage information flows so freely that most ardent followers get their scoops from Web sites as the news happens.

To be sure, a lot has changed when it comes to information and exposure. Today, wrestlers are everywhere. The Rock sat next to President George W. Bush at the Republican National Convention in 1999. Chyna and Sable were once *Playboy* magazine cover models. It's not unusual to see mainstream personalities like Jay Leno of "The Tonight Show," comedian Jimmy Kimmel, country crooner Toby Keith, and should-be Hall of Fame baseball player Pete Rose appear on wrestling television programs. In fact, wrestlers themselves are regarded as mainstream. The WWE has earned gold records with its music CDs, and The Rock has been in box-office-hit motion pictures.

Despite the dwindling media snub, we can't deny wrestling's firm connection to pop culture. It may appear to only be a modern-times spectacle, but wrestling has always been embedded in pop culture. In Mexico, El Santo and the Blue Demon made countless movies between them, and were

Known for his dropkick, Antonino Rocca sends Verne Gagne flying.

treated like gods by the public. East Coast legend Antonino Rocca cut an album in the 1950s. Minneapolis' Verne Gagne once hawked vitamins in 1960s. In Japan, the popular Tiger Mask wrestling character was actually derived from a children's cartoon program. You name it, when it comes to professional wrestlers, they truly have done it all.

Whatever your background, wrestling has made its impact on your soul. The young watch in hypnotic-like wonderment. Older folks watch with a childlike faith. There are no stereotypical wrestling fans. In Japan, many high-society members grab the front row seats similar to the chosen few who are invited to the opening of a Broadway play. The only difference between all of us lies in the passion. For some, being a fan is enough. However, there are those daring few who are bitten by the wrestling bug and become collectors, writers, promoters, referees, photographers, announcers, part of the ring crew, or Webmasters. A few even don the tights and become wrestlers themselves.

The mystery is what draws us in. In reality, every fan knew that Bruiser Brody could beat a wimpy foe like Greg Gagne into a bloody pulp and that Undertaker never was really resurrected from the dead. Despite reality telling us differently, we cheered anyway. Deep down, few fans believed the scrawny Bob Backlund could hold back the cadre of 400-pound challengers sent from eerie places by their evil managers, the Grand Wizard and Fred Blassie, to challenge his championship. But we chose to make believe. Most knew the Road Warriors and Abdullah the Butcher were fellow human beings, but none of us wanted to believe we could see them at the local grocery store. Perhaps that was, and still is, the beauty of professional wrestling, and why we're all fans.

Editor's note:

This book is intended to provide you with a great trip down memory lane. It must be said that there are many great wrestlers who deserve to have been included in this work, but could not be, due to space constraints. We hope you will enjoy our tribute to the good, the bad, and the unforgettable wrestlers who helped make this sport what it is today—one of the hottest forms of entertainment in the world.

Former WWF champ
Mankind (Mick Foley).

SLAMOGRAPHIES

Abdullah the Butcher
(1960s-2000s)

The scarred forehead is unmistakably Abby. This five-decade star is truly a legend. Born in Montreal and a world traveler ten times over, he's frightened opponents and fans while leaving a wide swath in his wake. His feuds with Bruiser Brody are classics. His never-ending mat journey continues today with stops at various independent shows across the United States.

Adams, Brian
(1990s-2000s)

Hawaii has been the origin of only a few competitors, and Adams still calls it home. He's had many opportunities to shine in WWF, WCW, and the Northwest. He's Antonio Inoki's son-in-law and was once the fourth member of Demolition. [Crush; Kronik]

Adonis, Adrian
(1970s-1980s)

A very solid technician who won world tag belts with Dick Murdoch (WWF) and Jesse Ventura (AWA), he had numerous runs as an East Coast bad boy. Later, he appeared in the WWF using a flamboyant homosexual gimmick. Adonis died in a 1988 car wreck. [Adorable Adrian]

Albano, Lou
(1950s-1980s)

Passers-by recognize Albano merely by the rubber bands dangling from his face. But Albano was a classic heel manager—after he was a WWWF tag champ with Tony Altimore in 1967—guiding the likes of the Samoans and Moondogs to tag belts.

Al-Kaissey, Adnan
(1960s-1990s)

Legitimate Iraqi native who played up his connection to Saddam Hussein in WWF storylines. He wrestled virtually every modern-era performer and was also a talented amateur, but is most known for managing Ken Patera, Crusher Blackwell, and Sgt. Slaughter. [Billy Whitewolf; General Adnan; Sheik Adnan]

Billy Whitewolf

Amish Roadkill
(1990s-2000s)

A grad of the Tazz's wrestling school, Roadkill is an agile big man with a quirky gimmick. He and Danny Doring were the last to hold the ECW tag belts.

Anderson, Arn
(1980s-2000s)

Marty Lunde was a preliminary attraction before he caught on as Ole Anderson's fictional nephew in the Mid-Atlantic area. One of the great tag-team wrestlers ever and an original member of the Four Horsemen, he won numerous world tag belts with Tully Blanchard. Injuries ended his career in 1999 and followed that stint as a WWE agent. [Super Olympia]

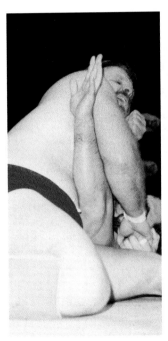

Anderson, Ole
(1960s-1990s)

Along with "brother" Gene, Alan Rogowski made up one-half of the original Minnesota Wrecking Crew. He wreaked havoc in NWA and Mid-Atlantic. A rugged performer who brought an air of believability, he later became a talent coordinator for Georgia Championship Wrestling. Later, he was a matchmaker for WCW and penned his autobiography, which included a scathing analysis of today's wrestling. [Black Scorpion]

Andre the Giant
(1960s-1990s)

A true legend in wrestling, during the 1970s, few wrestlers had more world-wide appeal than Andre. A Frenchman, he toured the world and was a special attraction in virtually every corner of the globe. His career climaxed in the 1987 Wrestlemania III main event against Hulk Hogan. He was also considered the King of the Battle Royals. [Eiffel Tower; Giant Machine; Giant Rouisimoff]

Andre the Giant, always gentle, shows jockey Bill Shoemaker what it's like to be over 7-feet tall.

Andre the Giant knew how to give the girls a lift.

Angle, Kurt
(1990s-2000s)

Former 1996 Olympic champion turned pro wrestler, Angle amazingly won every major WWE singles title in his rookie year in 2000. The Pittsburgh native is one of the fastest improving wrestlers ever and is as funny on the mike as he is skilled in the ring. He overcame a near career-ending injury in 2003 and returned to the spotlight to regain championships. He's long been rumored to be yearning for a return to legit fighting, like UFC, but his staus as a WWE star now appears cemented

Anthony, Tony
(1970s-2000s)

Part old-school, part hardcore, this Southerner had deep roots in Tennessee wrestling. This rugged, all-out brawler was one-half of the Dirty White Boys with Lynn Denton. He's shed blood in Continental, Northwest, Smoky Mountain, and Mid-South all the while, retaining his rough exterior. [Dirty White Boy; T.L. Hopper; Uncle Cletus]

Arakawa, Mitsu
(1950s-1960s)

Japanese star who performed in the Midwest and teamed with Mr. Moto to win AWA titles in 1967. Also teamed with Kinji Shibuya in the Midwest and Vancouver areas. In 1969, he held the WWWF International tag title with Toru Tanaka. He's one of the first Japan-born talents to find long-term success on U.S. soil.

Armstrong, Bob
(1970s-2000s)

This former fireman loved wrestling enough to leave a week before his pension was secured to become a ring star and molded himself into an icon in the Southeast region. He often moonlighted as the masked "Bullet" in many story lines, but to his enemy's frustration and fan's delight, everyone knew he was Bob. He is the father of wrestlers Brad, Steve, James, and Scott Armstrong. [The Bullet]

Armstrong, Jesse James
(1980s-2000s)

Brian James toiled in Memphis for years before catching a break as Jeff Jarrett's lackey. Then, in 1997, he created the totally unique Road Dogg character and tore the house down with his trademark quotes to win WWF tag titles with Billy Gunn. Since 2000, his career has received renewed attention in TNA, teaming with Konnan and others. [B.G. James; Roadie; Road Dogg]

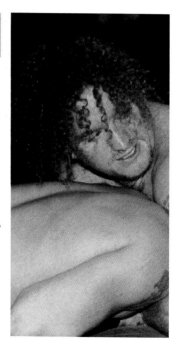

Atlas, Tony
(1970s-1990s)

This former smiling, bodybuilding freak was a main event star in NWA, WWF, and AWA rings, winning titles virtually everywhere he went. While he wasn't the greatest wrestler, his sculpted physique made him a memorable attraction. [Saba Simba; Superman]

Austin Idol
(1970s-1990s)

The Florida-based muscleman was often called a smaller version of Billy Graham, but Idol said different. He claims Hulk Hogan stole his own "Idolmania" and turned it into "Hulkamania," although no one knows for sure. But Idol was quite a star in the South during the 1980s. A gifted talker, he helped draw massive crowds to Memphis for his matches against Jerry Lawler in 1987. Although he never became a national star, Idol was a super regional performer. [Mick McCord]

Austin, Steve
(1980s-2000s)

A former blond-haired brawler, Austin broke onto the scene in Dallas in the late 1980s in a feud with his former trainer, Chris Adams. His breakout year was 1993 in WCW when he won the U.S. and tag-team titles. He toiled there until 1995 when the WWF took a chance on him. After an ill-fated push under the management of Ted DiBiase, he carved his own niche as "Stone Cold." Bringing a new style to wrestling, he ushered in a new era for the WWF. The former WWF champion's huge money feuds with Rock and Vince McMahon have cemented his place in history. [Ringmaster; Stunning Steve]

Awesome, Mike
(1980s-2000s)

A highly unusual wrestler. At close to 7-feet tall, he is huge, but maneuvers like a cruiserweight and has a penchant for high-risk moves. Between shots in WWF and WCW, he's been established in Japan for almost a decade and is also a former two-time ECW champion. Backstage politics likely derailed his chances of becoming a more noted star. [That 70s Guy; Gladiator]

Baba, Shohei "Giant"
(1960s-1990s)

One of the true legends of wrestling. A former baseball player, he was a student of Rikidozan in the 1960s. His 7-foot stature made him an instant hit. As the owner of All-Japan wrestling, he was a three-decade headliner. His success followed him to North America where he was a three-time NWA world champion. His passing in 1999 from cancer ended an era, but as the wide audience that watched his funeral on live television shows, he won't be forgotten. [Giant Baba]

Baby Doll
(1980s)

Longtime World Class and NWA valet who guided Dusty Rhodes and Tully Blanchard in some explosive early 1980s feuds. Sporting a Pat Benatar look, she was a sex object for the times. She later married wrestler Sam Houston.

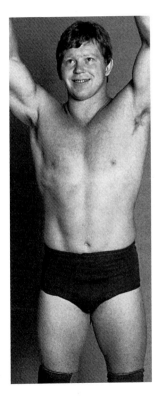

Backlund, Bob
(1980s-1990s)

Backlund, a stellar amateur, trained in the same camp as Jesse Ventura. When his career finally brought him to New York, he found himself in a strange situation: being on the small side, he was given the world title after the WWF fans were used to monsters like Billy Graham and Bruno Sammartino. Backlund made the opportunity work and finished as a three-time WWF world champion. He had epic feuds with Ken Patera and Don Muraco, which sold out Madison Square Garden. In later years, he turned to politics.

Baker, Ox
(1950s-1980s)

Stop the presses! The famous Ox is one of the scariest looking men to don the tights. If his looks didn't kill, his heart punch did—in 1972, Ray Gunkel died after injuries apparently suffered from Baker's punch. The Ox traveled far and wide as a main event star in the U.S., Canada, and Puerto Rico, but his career never culminated in world title reigns. He also had a role in the flick, "Escape from New York," upon his retirement.

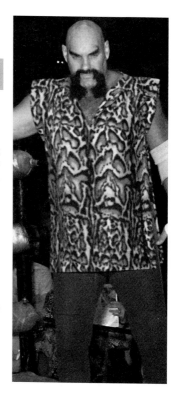

Bambi
(1980s-2000s)

The tanned Southern Belle has toured relentlessly around the country, but her biggest challenge has been finding opponents. She's headlined in various women's promotions like LPWA and WOWW. [Selina Majors]

Banner, Penny
(1950s-1970s)

This ladies' wrestler was a top challenger for the world title. A true athlete, this blonde bomber was the first AWA women's champion and, after retirement, has been active in the Senior Olympics. She even claims to have dated Elvis Presley in her younger days.

Barr, Art
(1980s-1990s)

Remembered as a rare American influence on Lucha Libre, this son of Portland promoter Sandy Barr was small in size, but was a buzz saw in the ring. When Roddy Piper crowned him with the Beetlejuice gimmick, Barr's career flourished. But it wasn't until he traveled to Mexico as Eddy Guerrero's partner that his true talents emerged. Before he could parlay his talent into American success, he died in 1994 at age 28. [Beetlejuice; Juicer; Love Machine]

Bassman, Rick
(1980s-2000s)

The California-based impresario brought Sting and Ultimate Warrior into the eyes of wrestling promoters through a group called Power Team USA. In the 1990s, he started recruiting future stars, such as John Cena, and promoted cards in Southern California in his UPW group.

Batista, Dave
(1990s-2000s)

The freaky looking bodybuilding phenom was a former OVW champion but got a call-up from the WWE and has patiently waited his turn. In 2005, he captured his first world title from Triple H and he could be the new face of WWE for many years to come. Batista is included in the hip group "Evolution" but his character evolved to a confident solo competitor. It's a departure from his early days when he toiled as a tag-team wrestler with partners D-Von Dudley and Randy Orton. [Deacon Batista; Leviathan]

Blears, James
(1950s-1980s)

The "Lord," as he was often known, was a distinguished British star who wrestled, announced, and promoted in Hawaii from the 1950s-70s. He also toured North America extensively. [Lord James Blears]

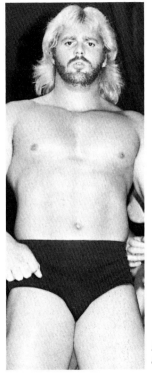

Beefcake, Brutus
(1980s-2000s)

Ed Leslie began his career as Hulk Hogan's phony cousin in Florida and that relationship served his career well. He reached superstar status in the 1980s as Brutus, winning the WWF tag title with Greg Valentine in 1985. A man of many identities, he overcame a tragic sailing accident that crushed every bone in his face. In his prime, he was a well-sculpted star who performed as a fan favorite and heel and later appeared in WCW as, you guessed it, a friend of Hogan's. [Barber; Butcher; Disciple; Ed Boulder; Man With No Name; Zodiac]

Brutus Beefcake in his days as Dizzy Ed Boulder.

Benoit, Chris
(1980s-2000s)

This wrestler from Canada adds an air of believability to the current scene. He trained under the Hart family tutelage in Calgary, but traveled the world to better his skills. A devoted follower of Dynamite Kid, he has emulated the former star's style and taken a nearly identical career path. Benoit's five-star matches in Mexico and Japan still have people raving. He's a former WWE and WCW world champ, and WWF tag-team and Intercontinental champion. [Wild Pegasus]

Berry, Red
(1930s-1950s)

"Wild" Red was one of the sport's first fanatical managers and famously guided the Fabulous Kangaroos team to stardom and championships around the country. Flamboyant to the end, he was a former boxer and light heavyweight wrestling champion before he turned to managing.

Big Daddy
(1960s-1980s)

Shirley Crabtree, a 300+-pound English wrestler, was a star in Europe in the 1970s and 1980s. The wrestler with a 64-inch chest had almost a cult following overseas. His persona was said to be a take-off of the late actor, Burl Ives. No doubt, people enjoyed his whimsical approach to wrestling.

Bigelow, Bam Bam
(1980s-2000s)

A former karate fighter, he considered shoot fighting and boxing careers before getting into wrestling through Larry Sharpe's Monster Factory in New Jersey. The agile, big man whose tattooed body led him to main events all over the country, has been a steady star—from his beginnings in World Class in the 1980s to the WCW and WWF in the late 1990s. [Beast from the East]

Blackwell, Jerry
(1970s-1990s)

No one ever said Blackwell looked like a wrestler, but he was one of the few 400 pounders who could move well in the ring. This talented brawler, who also held his own against the technicians, was a main event star in the AWA where he feuded with Mad Dog Vachon. He passed away in 1995 at age 45. [Crusher Blackwell]

Blanchard, Joe
(1960s-1990s)

After his wrestling career was finished, Blanchard was a successful promoter of Southwest Championship Wrestling out of San Antonio. The group, remembered as a blood and guts free-for-all, ran from 1970-85 before it was sold to the Von Erich family in Dallas. Joe, the father of Tully Blanchard, was also an AWA figurehead commissioner in the early 1990s.

Blanchard, Tully
(1970s-2000s)

He was a second-generation star and despite his diminutive size, was championship caliber. The former college football star held many regional titles including the Southwest belt eight times. Known as a tight fighter who could brawl and chain wrestle, his famous move was the slingshot suplex. He reached wide acclaim with the Horsemen in the 1980s. Together, with Arn Anderson, he was a three-time world tag-team champion. Blanchard retired from the ring before his prime ended to focus on ministry work but he has crept back into it as an independent performer in the South.

Blassie, Freddie
(1950s-2000s)

"Classy" Freddie Blassie: will forever be known in wrestling. Americans knew him as the "Hollywood fashion plate" and Japanese fans knew him as the "Vampire." Blassie did it all: records, television shows, stunt work, tours, you name it. His feuds with John Tolos, the Destroyer, and Rikidozan were historic. He toured the U.S. in the 1950s, including Los Angeles, and later he pushed the envelope in Japan. Seen in Dracula poses, he was known to bite his opponents. After retirement, he switched to managing and coined the nickname, "pencil-necked geek." In 2003, Blassie passed away.

Bloom, Wayne
(1980s-1990s)

The tall, tough guy was a former AWA world tag-team champion with fellow Minnesotan Mike Enos. A blond-haired tough talker, he was a marginal wrestler, but found decent success in the AWA, NWA, and WWF as a tag-team performer. [Beau Beverly]

Blue Demon
(1940s-1980s)

In Mexico, few wrestlers have had the type of success that the mask-wearing Demon had. A star in both the ring and in movies, his friendship with El Santo only went so far. In the ring, he and Santo were bitter enemies who drew monster crowds in the 1970s. He feuded with Santo over the NWA welterweight title, which he held solidly during a 4-1/2-year span. Blue Demon retired in 1989, but his legacy is strong—it is also followed by his son, who wrestles as Blue Demon Jr.

Bockwinkel, Nick
(1960s-1990s)

Few wrestlers have brought the
veracity for words as this second-
generation star. One of the more
technically sound performers
of any era, Bockwinkel was a
four-time AWA champion in the
1980s and a longtime tag-team
companion of Ray Stevens. The
duo won the AWA tag titles three
times. As smooth as he was in
the ring, he was smoother in
interviews in which he'd wrap up
his opponent's flaws with wit as
spectacular as his wrestling holds.

A younger Nick Bockwinkel in action.

Boesch, Paul
(1940s-1980s)

Not many people
can boast the life of
Paul Boesch. A wrestler,
promoter, announcer,
WWII soldier, and author,
Boesch was a favorite
promoter of many
wrestlers. His wild and
wooly Houston-area
shows, which often
featured cross-promotion
champions, pioneered
famous gimmick matches
still used today. Boesch
died in 1989.

Booker T.
(1990s-2000s)

Trained in Texas by Ivan Putski and Scott Casey, Booker grew from the independents to become only the second African American WCW world champion in history, a belt he carried five times. A very gifted and athletic star, he's the real-life brother of Stevie Ray, who he held the WCW tag title with 10 times. He's become a popular WWE singles star, often challenging for that group's world title. [G.I. Bro]

Bossman, The
(1980s-2000s)

A surprisingly agile man, he began his career as Bubba Rogers, a bodyguard for manager Jim Cornette, but his talent in the ring would emerge later. He was tendered an offer to wrestle in the WWF as the Bossman and his career took off. While not a championship type, he has been a headliner in the WWF and WCW. He died in 2004, at age 42, of a heart attack. [Big Bubba Rogers; Guardian Angel; Ray Traylor]

Boyd, Jonathan
(1970s-1980s)

As one of the founding Sheepherders, the ugly faced Boyd was an anti-American heat-seeker throughout the country, most notably in the Southwest and Northwest. A fan of blood and barbed wire, he survived a debilitating car accident to resume his career.

Boyette, Mike
(1960s-1980s)

This wrestler appeared as a California hippie wearing beaded vests. Seen in the Gulf Coast region, he even had a series against the legendary Danny Hodge, which showed the serious and talented side of his career which was often overlooked. He once held the U.S. tag-team title.

Bradshaw
(1990s-2000s)

The West Texas native harkens to the days of Stan Hansen. He played college football and tried wrestling just as Hansen did. A very large character, he searched for a role in the WWF. As Ron Simmons' partner, they won the WWF tag titles three times. By 2000 his connection to Hansen bloomed. As the tough man Bradshaw, he captured WWE gold. He also adopted the JR Ewing-like JBL persona, but he's never strayed from his roots. [Blackjack Bradshaw; John Hawk; Justin Hawk, JBC]

Brazil, Bobo
(1940s-1980s)

One of the few wrestlers to perform for more than five decades, this African-American star was very influential in breaking color barriers. Some reports have him turning pro in 1939 and wrestling into the 1990s, which would make him a seven-decade vet. A native of Benton Harbor, Mich., and master of the coconut headbutt, he was a classy champion in the Detroit area and gave that belt respect. He had famous, bloody feuds with Johnny Valentine, Killer Kowalski, Fred Blassie, and the Sheik.

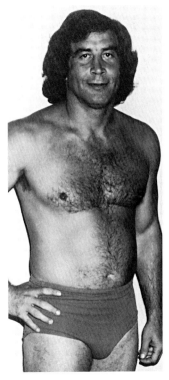

Brisco, Jack
(1960s-1980s)

This multi-talented athlete and wrestler was one of the prides of the 1970s. A former NCAA champion in 1965 at Oklahoma State, he held the NWA world title two times between 1973-75. He dethroned Harley Race and Giant Baba for the crown. A true fighting champion, he defended the title on a six-day-a-week schedule. Outside his title defenses, he and his brother, Jerry, had a career-long feud with the Texas Funk family.

The multi-talented Jack Brisco.

Brisco, Jerry
(1960s-2000s)

Like his brother Jack, he was a talented wrestler in his day, winning three NWA tag-team titles with his brother. The Oklahoma-born Briscos were part Native American. After his wrestling career, Jerry became a valued employee with the WWF, working as a road agent, in addition to his infamous Brisco's Body Shop in Florida.

Brody, Bruiser
(1970s-1980s)

One of the hardcore innovators, no fan or wrestler was safe when the 6-foot-8, longhaired wild man was present. A true rebel, Brody was never around any territory long enough to look bad. Born in west Texas, he was a college football player but went to wrestling for the money. In Japan, Brody's status is legendary. As a single's competitor, he drew incredible crowds for matches with Antonio Inoki. He teamed regularly with Jimmy Snuka and Stan Hansen against the top Japanese attractions. Tragically, Brody died from stab wounds in 1988 while on tour in Puerto Rico. [Red River Jack]

Brunzell, Jim
(1970s-1990s)

This skilled high-flyer
made his debut in 1972
and had a very productive
career in the AWA, WWF, and
Japan. Tag-team wrestling
was Brunzell's forte. As the
partner of Greg Gagne, the
duo was called the High
Flyers and won the AWA
tag titles two times. In the
1980s, Brunzell sported a
Bruce Springsteen look and
even recorded a takeoff on
one of the pop star's songs
called "Matlands." He then
crossed to the WWF, where
he teamed with B. Brian
Blair as the Killer Bees.

Bundy, King Kong
(1980s-1990s)

Bundy was a bald, towering presence who, at 400 pounds, was quite speedy. One of his gimmicks was to give opponents a fair chance by allowing a five-count, rather than the traditional three-count. In his prime, he toured virtually every major territory, but was made famous in the WWF for five-plus years. He even challenged Hulk Hogan for the world title in a cage bout at Wrestlemania II.

Burke, Leo
(1960s-1970s)

One of Canada's top junior heavyweights, he carried Calgary's British Commonwealth belt. He didn't avoid the big boys, however, and was a seven-time Calgary heavyweight champion.

Burke, Mildred
(1930s-1950s)

This former women's champion lays claim to more than 5,000 wins against women—and 150 wins against men. A tremendous athlete, her physique was quite unique. She was 5-foot-2, but incredibly toned and strong. Her career began on the carnival tours but it took her around the world many times.

Calhoun, Haystacks
(1960s-1970s)

One of the top draws of the 1960s, Calhoun was a pure oddity because of his size. The 600-pounder wore overalls and a scruffy beard. His freakish appeal made him an attraction throughout the world. In pre-cable television days, Calhoun was a must-see and made headlines in the WWWF in a feud with Bruno Sammartino. Photos of Bruno body slamming Calhoun appeared in several American newspapers. He and Tony Garea held the company's tag-team titles in 1973. His poor diet and training habits took a toll and before he passed away, diabetes took his leg.

Cameron, Larry
(1980s-1990s)

The former Canadian Football League player had a career in bodybuilding before hitting the rings in the Midwest. Not known on a wide scale in the U.S., Cameron was the last wrestler to hold the Calgary Stampede heavyweight title before the promotion closed. He was a part-time member of WCW's tag-team champions, Doom. While on tour in Germany in 1993, Cameron died; it was later attributed to heart failure.

Canadian Wildman
(1970s-1980s)

Dave McKigney, sporting a beard, looked like a wildman, hence the gimmick. An outlaw wrestler in Canada, he trained novelty wrestling bears and often performed against them in the ring. He wrote the cult book, Drawing Heat. He died in 1988 in a car accident that also took the lives of Adrian Adonis and Pat Kelly. [Bearman]

Candido, Chris
(1990s-2000s)

A former holder of the NWA championship, Candido broke off from the East Coast independent groups to get shots in Smoky Mountain, WCW, and WWF. Along with Tom Pritchard in the Body Donna's tag team, he won the WWF tag title in 1996. The life partner of Tammy Sytch, he fought a drug addiction and seemed to be clean and ready for Act II in TNA when he died suddenly in 2005, from complications from surgery at age 33. [Skip]

Cannon, George
(1950s-1980s)

The "Crybaby" was a wrestler, manager, announcer, and promoter—and he was skilled at all. Best known for his work in Detroit's Big Time Wrestling, the 300-pound Cannon got his nickname from throwing tantrums and "crying" after losses.

Carpentier, Edouardo
(1950s-1980s)

Nicknamed the "Flying Frenchman," Carpentier was a strapping high-flyer who used his experience in gymnastics in the ring to delight crowds. He was one of the first to complete somersaults from the top ropes and land on his foes. He held many titles in his prime, including several branches of the world title. He even beat Lou Thesz for the NWA world title in 1957, but the title change was later reversed. His deep career took him into the 1980s in Canada and he also served as a wrestling television commentator. His nephew, Jacky Weicz, also wrestled using the Carpentier name.

Castillo, Hurricane
(1960s-1980s)

The Puerto Rican wrestler was one of the first major stars on the island. He held numerous belts, including the NWA Caribbean title and WWC Universal title. He found early success in Montreal in the 1960s, where he was a top heel teaming with Abdullah the Butcher. His son also wrestles as Hurricane Castillo Jr. [Fidel Castillo]

Cena, John
(1990s-2000s)

Cena proved good things happen to people who want it badly enough. The Boston-native had dreams of becoming champion one day. He started as a student in Rick Bassman's California group but was quickly snatched up by the WWF. He spent time as the OVW champion in Louisville before heading to the big show, where he showed the charisma needed to go far. Boy has he. He embraced a questionable rapper gimmick and made it his. Fans caught on and ultimately embraced Cena. In 2005, he captured his first world title. He's said publicly his priorities are to wrestling, not Hollywood. Fans can only hope that's the case. [Prototype]

Chono, Masa
(1980s-2000s)

There is no denying his success in Japan, but Chono was one of the few to "get" American wrestling. He brought that style back to Japan in the 1990s. He broke into the business with Keiji Mutoh and later feuded with him. He wasn't a stranger to championships either: he's a former two-time NWA champ, one-time IWGP champion, and six-time IWGP tag-team champion.

Choshu, Ricky
(1970s-1990s)

One of the recent legends in Japan, Choshu rose through the pros stemming from his standout amateur career which took him to the 1972 Olympic Games. Into the 1980s, he became one of the country's most explosive performers and helped establish Japan's strong style of wrestling. A longtime front office employee in New Japan Wrestling, he's held many world titles, including the IWGP belt three times.

Christanello, Donna
(1960s-1980s)

One of the few female journeymen in wrestling, she was co-holder of the WWF women's tag-team title with Toni Rose in 1970.

Fabulous Moolah has her hands full with Donna Christanello.

Christian
(1990s-2000s)

This Canadian independent star got a shot in the WWE, and made the best of it. Christian employs a classic style and remains one of the more talented workers around. He is a former seven-time tag-team champion with Edge. The duo hit its stride in the late 1990s in a series of ladder matches against the Hardy Boys and he has made a name on the singles circuit. Not to be sold short, he has bettered himself into one of the more reliable and entertaining heels going. [Christian Cage]

Chyna
(1990s-2000s)

Brawny and powerful, Chyna is perhaps the most successful WWF female of all-time. Carefully promoted, she never wrestled women until later in her tour. She burst on the scene as a bodyguard, but eventually became one of the group's most recognizable faces. The only female to hold a men's WWF major championship, she beat Jeff Jarrett for the Intercontinental title in 1999, a belt she held twice. [Joanie Laurer]

Clark, Bryan
(1980s-2000s)

At 275 pounds and nearly 6-foot-7, the wrestling industry is a perfect home for a guy like Clark. He's found homes in the AWA, Smoky Mountain, WCW, and WWF. Using mainly power moves, Clark has wrestled almost exclusively as a heel. His major chance as champion came as the partner of Brian Adams in WCW. Together, the duo were two-time tag champions. [Adam Bomb; Night Stalker; Wrath]

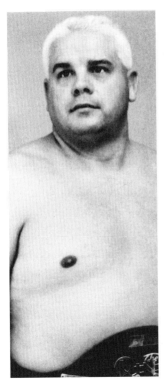

Collins, Ripper
(1950s-1980s)

Remembered as a vicious heel, Collins made Hawaii his home and often teamed with the equally demonic King Curtis. He held the Hawaiian Heavyweight title seven times from 1969-71. Later in his career, Collins tamed a bit and became a TV announcer.

Colon, Carlos
(1960s-2000s)

One name is synonymous with Puerto Rico: Colon. This head of the family never reached fame globally but it wasn't for his lack of trying. He tried his hand on the mainland but success always eluded him. He's been an island hero since the 1960s, most often carrying the World Wrestling Council title. In recent years, Colon was still active, often helping his children, Eddie, Carly, and Stacey, with ring careers of their own. [Carlos Belafonte]

Combs, Cora
(1960s-1980s)

One of the modern-day travelers, Combs, a first-generation star from the 1970s, was once billed as the women's U.S. champion. She toured the world to find competition, and often battled the best counterparts of the day.

Combs, Debbie
(1980s-1990s)

The daughter of Cora Combs, she was a journeyman wrestler in the 1980s with visits in virtually every major territory. Some of her tours took her to the WWF where she challenged Fabulous Moolah for the world women's title.

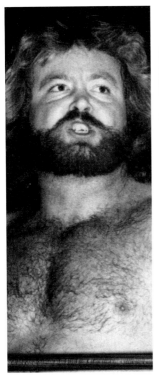

Condrey, Dennis
(1970s-1990s)

A true Southerner, Condrey found a home in Tennessee in his early years but was nothing more than a bit player before he hooked up with Randy Rose as the Midnight Express. When Jim Cornette finally got a hold of the team, Rose was replaced with Bobby Eaton and Condrey's career blossomed. In the early 1980s, Condrey toured World Class, Mid-South, and the NWA, where he was a U.S. and world tag-team champion. Later, he rejoined Rose in the AWA and won that group's tag championship.

Constantino, Rico
(1990s-2000s)

Something of a renaissance man, Rico was a former Las Vegas cop who competed on the TV show, "American Gladiators." In his mid-30s, he tried pro wrestling on a whim. He competed in OVW for several years and his dedication to improving was rewarded when he was offered a WWF contract in 2001. He's been both OVW champion and Southern tag-team champion with John Cena. Although his Adrian Street-like gimmick was good for laughs, it was not enough to keep his spot on the roster. [Rico]

Conway, Rob
(1990s-2000s)

Nicknamed the "Ironman," Conway is a former Ohio Valley Wrestling heavyweight champion. He was a key member of that promotion and favorite of promoter Danny Davis. Then Conway received the call up to the WWE and underwent a nationality change, aligning with Sylvain Grenier, with whom he won tag title gold. [Robert Conway]

Cornette, Jim
(1970s-2000s)

The insanely witty Cornette began his career as a wrestling photojournalist in Memphis and Louisville but quickly turned his attention to managing. For the following 20 years, he was one of the industry's highest-profile managers, guiding the likes of the Midnight Express, Bubba Rogers, and Yokozuna in World Class, Mid-South, Memphis, the NWA, and WWF. Often called too old school for his own good, Cornette has stood by his convictions as a wrestling promoter in the now defunct Smoky Mountain territory, as well as Ohio Valley Wrestling. Now with his managerial career over, he has great value as a talent developer, a roll he truly relishes.

Credible, Justin
(1980s-2000s)

Often deemed too small, Credible worked many different gimmicks before settling on this persona. He was a minor hit in the WWF and Memphis but received his big break in ECW. There, he had a six-month run as world champion. He was also a two-time ECW tag champion with Lance Storm. [Aldo Montoya; Man of War; P.J. Walker]

Crockett Jr., Jim
(1970s-1980s)

The oldest son of Crockett Sr., he took over the promotional reigns of the Mid-Atlantic area from his father in 1973 and ran it until he sold the group to Ted Turner in 1988. He was a three-time president of the NWA. Gone from wrestling (despite another failed attempt to promote in the early 90s), he resides in Dallas.

Crockett Sr., Jim
(1930s-1970s)

Patriarch of one of the famous names in North American wrestling history, he promoted the Carolinas and Virginia from 1935-73 until his oldest son took over the family business. For years, his name was synonymous with wrestling. He was an integral member of the NWA. The true measure of his contribution is the fact that, even today, people recall the Crockett name.

Crush Gals, The
(1980s-1990s)

A famous name in Japanese women's wrestling, this team, comprised of Lioness Asuka and Chigusa Nagayo, were superstars. They had a classic feud with Dump Matsumoto and Bull Nakano and won the WWWA tag titles three times.

Crusher, The
(1950s-1980s)

A complete master of mayhem, Reggie Lisowski was a main event star throughout the world but is most known in the Midwest where his career finished in the early 1980s. At the height of his career, he was a barrel-chested brawler who drove fans wild in the 1950s and 1960s and later he became a popular fan favorite. He feuded feverishly against Mad Dog Vachon and Baron Von Raschke. The innovator of the stomach claw and bolo punch, he was known for his trademark cigars and hilarious interviews.

Curry, Wild Bull
(1950s-1970s)

Born of Lebanese descent, he was a pure wild man in the ring and incited many crowd riots. He made a name for himself in Texas, where he was a constant in the Houston area's Brass Knuckles division. He once boxed Jack Dempsey. Fans from his day still remember his wild, overgrown eyebrows.

BULL CURRY

BULL CURRY

Curtis, Don
(1950s-1970s)

The "Buffalo Bomber" was said to have been discovered by Lou Thesz. Not too shabby. He was a two-time U.S. tag champ with Mark Lewin and he also held the WWWF tag title. Later, he promoted in Florida.

Daniels, Christopher
(1990s-2000s)

A very talented East Coast indy wrestler, Daniels is a technically sound attraction. He's found success in Japan, as well as Ring of Honor and NWA-TNA. [Curry Man; Fallen Angel]

Darsow, Barry
(1980s-2000s)

A man of many
identities, Darsow carved
a nice career out of being
a mid-level gimmick
performer. He spent
some time in Mid-South
before catching on with
the Crockett's in Georgia.
Promoters put him in
many roles, but his most
famous was as one half of
Demolition, a copy of the
Road Warriors. Together
with Bill Eadie, the face-
painted Darsow won the
WWF tag-team title three
times. [Blacktop Bully;
Demolition Smash; Krusher
Kruschev; Repo Man.]

Davis, Mike
(1970s-2000s)

Davis began his career as a light heavyweight and was considered a fine worker. As wrestling boomed in the 1980s, Davis formed the RPMs with various partners. They were very active in the Southeast and Puerto Rico. After nearly 25 years on the road, he passed away in 2001. [Maniac Mike; Viper.]

Heyman photo

DeBeers, Col.
(1980s-1990s)

After learning his craft in Portland as a technician, he entered the AWA as a brawling colonel. Billed as a member of a South African diamond mining family, he had high profile feuds against Sgt. Slaughter and Derrick Dukes. Yet most of his money-making days were in Portland where he enjoyed a 10-year run in the regional hotbed. [Ed Wiskoski; Mega Maharishi]

Del Rey, Jimmy
(1980s-1990s)

A smallish, Tennessee-based wrestler who wrestled around the Southeast and later teamed with Tom Pritchard as the Heavenly Bodies in Smoky Mountain Wrestling. The tandem was multi-time SMW tag champs. [Gigolo; Jimmy Backlund]

Ax striking a pose.

Demolition
(1980s-1990s)

Vince McMahon needed a quick answer to the Road Warriors who were tearing up the NWA in 1986. His answer seemed simple: copy them. McMahon put Barry Darsow and Bill Eadie in face paint, spikes, and leather and called them Demolition. At first fans weren't fooled. But in time, the Demos created their own identity, were given lengthy runs as world tag champs, and performed admirably. In history, the Roadies are legendary, but at the time, WWF fans were none the wiser.

DeMott, Bill
(1990s-2000s)

A stocky brawler in WCW and WWE who seemed to take a page from Jim Duggan's early style of wrestling. He even bore a resemblance to Duggan. He's a two-time U.S. champion. Following his ring career, DeMott was a decent TV announcer for the WWE. [Capt. Rection; Hugh Morrus]

Diamond Lil
(1970s)

This was one of the few female midget wrestlers. She toured the country, but had few opponents.

Diamond, Paul
(1980s-1990s)

He was a former pro soccer player from Florida before he headed for the gym to wrestle. He held numerous tag titles with Pat Tanaka and was one-half of Badd Company and the Orient Express. His career took him regionally to Florida and Memphis and then to TV promotion and the AWA and WWF before finding a way back to the Indy circuit. [Kato; Maxx Moon]

DiBiase, Ted
(1980s-1990s)

Few wrestlers have the fluidity in the ring like this second-generation star. Long before he was the WWF's Million Dollar Man, he was a gritty fan-fave Mid-South champ. With the millionaire gimmick, he totally lived the part, flying private jets and riding in limos. But he was worth it. DiBiase was a phenomenal in-ring talent. Although he never got credit for it, his feuds with Hogan and Savage were classics, mainly due to him. [Million Dollar Man]

Dick the Bruiser
(1950s-1980s)

Havoc was the middle name for this rugged ex-football player. He often partnered with the Crusher through the Midwest and co-ran the Indianapolis-based WWA. In the 1960s and 1970s, there weren't many wrestlers who created mayhem like the Bruiser. He died in 1991.

Dillon, J.J.
(1970s-2000s)

As a wrestler and manager, Dillon did his best to rile fans. Ironically, the former manager of the Four Horsemen is one of the most respected men in wrestling. He won numerous regional titles as an adequate wrestler, but his true claim to fame was guiding the Horsemen, the pioneering NWA group of wrestlers led by Ric Flair. Since his ringside days ended, Dillon has been a big influence backstage in WWF, WCW, and NWA-TNA.

DiPaolo, Ilio
(1950s-1960s)

Born in Italy, DiPaolo found a surrogate home in Buffalo, where he remains a legend. He overcame polio as a youth to become an athletic star. For most of his career, he was a solid mid-card attraction on the East Coast, but he had flashes of brilliance: among them, a Canadian tag title stint with Whipper Watson and two, 60-minute title bout draws against Pat O'Connor and Lou Thesz.

DiSalvo, Steve
(1980s)

Not all visually impressive stars were successful and DiSalvo showed that. Trained by Californian Bill Anderson, the former Calgary champion had the looks of a superstar, but he ended up as one of wrestling's powerhouse flops. He had brief opportunities in the AWA, WWF, and Puerto Rico, where he was the Universal champion in 1989. He's a talented painter, too, and was commissioned to paint Jesse Ventura's official portrait for the state of Minnesota as former Governor. [Billy Jack Strong; Steve Strong]

Douglas, Shane
(1980s-2000s)

Widely known for his role as the Franchise in ECW, Douglas is a journeyman who also holds a teaching degree. Always a great interview, he helped build a young ECW into a national promotion. He wrestled in many territories after getting his first break with Bill Watts' UWF. From his younger days as a high-flyer to his ECW world title run, Douglas always fit the bill. [Dean Douglas; Franchise]

Downtown Bruno
(1980s-2000s)

This pal of Jerry Lawler got a chance in Memphis where he became another in the line of funny heel managers there. He guided virtually every heel to come through the area during the late 1980s. He went to WWF, where he had a major run as manager of champion, Psycho Sid. Never adverse to wrestling himself when needed, he actually held the WWE women's title for one day after beating the Kat. [Harvey Wippleman]

Dreamer, Tommy
(1990s-2000s)

An ECW legend who has left blood on mats around the country, he was a softy when all of a sudden, the hardcore style hit him like a brick. He had a quiet and controlled, yet crazy, demeanor. He won and lost the ECW title on the same show in 2000. [T.D. Madison]

Dudley Boys, The

(1990s-2000s)

When the Public Enemy departed ECW, Paul Heyman created this strange gimmick, but it worked. Originally D-Von and Bubba Ray, there were many more Dudleys that popped in, including Dances with Wolves Dudley, Dudley Dudley and Sign Guy Dudley. The original two, who could brawl to no end, held numerous tag-team titles and have gone on to greater heights in the WWF.

Duggan, Jim
(1980s-2000s)

Three careers make up this Buffalo native's ring life: First, he was a terrific brawler in Bill Watts' Mid-South and UWF in the early 1980s; then, he took the money and had a great run as a comedy act in the WWF; later, he's been a part-time performer who can still get pops from crowds who remember his years on top of his game. In 2000, he showed his courage in a return to the ring after a fight with cancer.

Dundee, Bill
(1970s-2000s)

Former Australian tightrope artist who became a wrestling star in Memphis in the late 1970s. He was a longtime foe and friend of Jerry Lawler and he's held numerous Mid-South singles and tag-team titles. At 5-5, he never turned down a challenge: he's known to go toe-to-toe with the likes of Terry Funk, Austin Idol, and Dutch Mantel. His son, Jamie, has carved a career for himself in the ring.

Duseks, The
(1930s-2000s)

Nebraska was home to this renegade wrestling family, led by renowned shooter, Wally Dusek. Wally and his brothers, Emil, Ernie, Rudy, and Joe, all wrestled from the 1930s to 1950s. For a time, they were called the notorious Omaha Riot Squad. Joe Dusek later promoted the city. Frank Dusek, the son of Wally, did it all in later years as a wrestler, promoter, and television producer in Texas.

Frank Dusek

Dynamite Kid
(1980s-1990s)

One of the most influential wrestlers of the modern era, Tom Billington helped usher in a style never seen before in North America. The style, learned in Canada, picked from the best from Mexico and Japan. He was a high-flying, suplex machine who was unafraid to hurt his body in the ring. Before he began teaming with Davey Boy Smith as the British Bulldogs, Dynamite was a star in Canada and Japan in the 1980s. He held the WWF tag championship with Smith for eight months. Sadly, his career was shut down from the incredible punishment he sustained through the years.

Eagle, Don
(1950s-1960s)

One of the sport's
true Native Americans,
Eagle was a very colorful
performer who brought
pride to his tribe, the
Mohawks. He appeared
around the U.S. and
Canada and even held the
AWA version of the world
title in 1950. In the ring,
he was successful, but his
inner demons caught up to
him in 1966 when he took
his own life.

Eaton, Bobby
(1970s-2000s)

Quiet and understated, Eaton was regarded as one of the best wrestlers of the 1980s. Technically superior to most of his contemporaries, his fame skyrocketed as one-half of the Midnight Express. Born in Huntsville, Ala., he grew up watching wrestling and graduated to setting up rings before he trained for the ring himself. He had brilliant stints in Mid-South, Dallas, and the NWA. He carried the NWA tag titles three times with three different partners (Dennis Condrey, Stan Lane, and Arn Anderson). [Earl Robert Eaton]

Edge
(1990s-2000s)

One of the breakout stars in the WWE, Adam Copeland carries on the pipeline of talent from Canada to the United States. He trained with Dory Funk Jr. after some time on the independent scene and quickly made an impact in the WWE. Very charismatic, he epitomizes the new style of wrestling. He's a four-time Intercontinental champion and seven-time tag-team champion with steady partner, Christian. [Sexton Hardcastle]

El Canek
(1960s-1990s)

The masked, high-flying Mexican star was one of the bigger draws in Lucha Libre history. The former UWA world champion had main events after Mil Mascaras departed for the U.S. in the 1970s. Canek is remembered as one of the few to beat Andre the Giant, which he did in 1984. Billed as the brother of Don Caras and Mil Mascaras, he was also a huge star in England and Japan.

The masked El Canek was a top draw.

El Santo
(1960s-1980s)

A true legend in wrestling, El Santo's role cannot be overlooked. He was a mega-star in Mexico and ushered in a new era of multimedia personalities. In the ring, he stands as the top drawing attraction of all-time. He also appeared in more than 80 feature films, which are still regarded as cult classics.

Elizabeth
(1980s-1990s)

No female played the "damsel in distress" better than Liz, who was a popular WWF ringside attraction in the 1980s. A onetime wife of wrestler Randy Savage, she was part of many super feuds alongside Savage. Later, she appeared in WCW, sometimes with Savage, who she was actually separated from in real life. Sadly, she died in 2003.

Embry, Eric
(1970s-1990s)

With a body never to be confused with a heavyweight, Embry's verbal skills took him around the regional territories of the 1980s. He also relied heavily on his skills as a scriptwriter, especially in Dallas, where he helped the USWA draw big crowds in the later part of the decade. A brawler and bleeder, he was a favorite to fans who enjoyed his underdog roles in the ring.

Equalizer, The
(1980s-1990s)

This Portland-based big man lacked pure wrestling skills but had a few decent runs. After his days in the old Northwest territory, where he teamed with the Grappler, he ventured to WCW before quitting the business. [Evad Sullivan]

Eugene
(1990s-2000s)

An energetic, young star from the Ohio Valley group, he held the company's championship and he's also been a long-time partner of Rob Conway. But Dinsmore wanted more. A theater teacher in Louisville, he was ready to quit when he was finally hired by the WWE. Vince McMahon gave him the persona Eugene, a mentally handicapped man with a perpetual smile. Due to his will—and his background in character acting, Eugene flourished in the WWE and was an immediate hit. [Nick Dinsmore]

Executioners, The
(1970s)

How do you hide an already known 300-pound star and one of the most recognizable bodies in wrestling history? Easy: put a mask on them. It seemed to be that type of logic when John Studd and Killer Kowalski won the WWWF tag-team titles in 1976 from Louis Cerdan and Tony Parisi. Never defeated in the ring, they were stripped of the belts because of the interference from a third partner, the masked Nikolai Volkoff.

The Fabulous Kangaroos: Roy Heffernan, Red Berry, and Al Costello.

Fabulous Kangaroos, The
(1960s-1970s)

Roy Heffernan and Al Costello founded this top-drawing tag team and later Don Kent was brought into replace Heffernan. Often managed by George Cannon, they had successful runs as the U.S. tag champions and defended those belts in Chicago, Detroit, and the Northeast.

Fabulous Moolah
(1940s-2000s)

A seven-decade performer, who is regarded as the queen of women's wrestling. Moolah held the WWF women's title from 1956 to 1984 and was wrestling well into the new millennium. [Slave Girl; Spider Lady]

**Fabulous
Ones, The
(1980s-1990s)**

After feuding against each other to marginal box office success, Steve Keirn and Stan Lane formed the "Fabs," managed by Jackie Fargo. Heading to the ring as Z.Z. Top's "Sharp Dressed Man" played on the loudspeakers and wearing top hats, the duo shot to stardom in Memphis and the AWA. Classic feuds ensued against the Sheepherders and Moondogs.

Fantastics, The
(1980s-1990s)

Tommy Rogers and Bobby Fulton were a top team in the 1980s in the Rock & Roll Express mold. Skilled technicians, they had memorable feuds with the Sheepherders and Midnight Express. While they had tours of most major territories in the 1980s, they always played second fiddle to the company's top teams.

Fargo, Jackie
(1950s-1980s)

An old-time legend in Louisville and Memphis, Jack Faggart was the leader of the Fabulous Fargo Bros. With beautiful blond manes and a flare for the dramatic, they were one of the South's best drawing teams ever. Jackie was a big-time heel teaming with Don Fargo. He also teamed with his brother, Roughhouse Sonny Fargo.

Finlay, Dave
(1980s-2000s)

Wrestlers don't come any more rugged than Finlay, an English-born wrestler who is known as a "stretcher" by many peers. His career was spent mostly in Europe, trading various belts with Tony St. Clair and Dave Taylor, but toward his later years, he hit the scene in WCW. While there, he suffered a devastating knee injury in a hardcore bout, but rehabilitated himself back to action. With WCW closed, he found a home in the WWE as a road agent. [Belfast Bruiser; Fit Finlay]

Firpo,
Pampero
(1950s-1980s)

Fans keenly remember the wild-haired maniac, who claimed he was from South America, keeping foreign objects in his mop hairdo. It was a heck of a gimmick. Firpo appeared all over the country including Hawaii, Texas, the AWA area, and Puerto Rico. [Ivan the Terrible]

Flair, David
(1990s-2000s)

It's always hard to live up to a family name, but David Flair really had great odds to beat: he's the real-life son of former world champion Ric Flair, who is perhaps the greatest of all-time. David, the eldest son, has been learning his craft. He has spent time in NWA Wildside, Ohio Valley Wrestling, and WCW, as well as NWA-TNA. He briefly made an appearance in WWF with his dad in his feud with the Undertaker, but the shoes might be too big to fill.

Flair, Ric
(1970s-2000s)

Often called the greatest wrestler ever, Flair has done it all and has held a world title more times (14) than anyone in history. He learned his craft in the Mid-Atlantic region and helped bridge the old school with the new during the 1980s. His charisma and ability to make opponents look great was unparalleled. He beat Dusty Rhodes for his first NWA world title in 1981. Flair, although born in Minnesota, is a legend in North Carolina, where he once considered running for governor. His many feuds included notable wrestlers Roddy Piper, Harley Race, and Hulk Hogan. [Black Scorpion; Nature Boy]

Ric Flair often showed up to the ring wearing fancy robes.

Flash Flannagan
(1990s-2000s)

A former Ohio Valley champ, the Mid-South star is an awesome hardcore risk-taker who has had difficulty being accepted as a television star. He has wrestled mainly in the Southern independents in Tennessee and Kentucky.

Foley, Mick
(1980s-2000s)

A former independent
mainstay, Foley bucked
conventional wisdom when
he earned a 1998 world
title run. Foley was a pudgy
journeyman before getting
his first break in WCW.
Known for risking his body,
he was never more than
a mid-card attraction. His
career veered to Japan and
the upstart ECW, where
he helped create a new
hardcore style. In the
WWF, he got his chance.
After wrestling with the
gimmick, Mankind, Foley
made his case while the
group needed new stars.
In feuds with the Rock
and Steve Austin, Mankind
touched the masses and
got three world title stints.
[Dude Love; Jack Foley;
Mankind; Super Zodiac No.
2, Cactus Jack]

Windham and Flair discuss strategy.

Four Horsemen, The
(1980s-1990s)

Some say the Horsemen, created in the NWA in 1983, marked the beginning of the groups of today. The originals were Tully Blanchard, Ole and Arn Anderson, and Ric Flair, with J.J. Dillon as their manager. The group changed in later years with others like Sid Vicious, Barry Windham, Paul Roma, and Chris Benoit joining in. Most of the time, the members held title belts, led by Flair and the NWA world championship.

Francine
(1990s)

Former Queen of Extreme in ECW, the mouthy brunette was the gal pal of Tommy Dreamer and also managed Shane Douglas and Justin Credible.

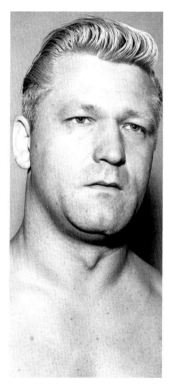

Francis, Ed
(1950s-1970s)

This former NWA junior heavyweight champion was a big name through the 1970s in Hawaii and helped promote there with Lord James Blears. Francis was a three-time Hawaii titleholder. At one time, because of Francis' help, wrestling on the island was the highest-rated television show on Saturday nights. His two sons, Bill and Russ, also wrestled.

Francis, Russ
(1970s-1980s)

The son of Ed Francis, Russ was a three-time Pro Bowl football player from the 1970s-80s. In 1985, the tight end helped San Francisco win a Super Bowl championship. Because of his dad's influence, Russ wrestled in the off-season to stay in shape, in Hawaii and Oregon, where he attended college. He also promoted briefly in Hawaii before running for public office on the islands.

Freebirds, The
(1970s-1990s)

Michael Hayes was ready to quit wrestling forever when fate stepped in. He took a ride with the equally frustrated Terry Gordy one night after a meager payoff and the two put their heads together and came up with the Freebirds gimmick. With the pesky Buddy Roberts, the trio was brash and groundbreaking. Hayes handled the mike, and Gordy, even as a teen, could wrestle circles around the vets. The threesome went on to heights in World Class against the Von Erichs and in Georgia against all comers and were a classic team.

Fuller, Buddy
(1950s-1970s)

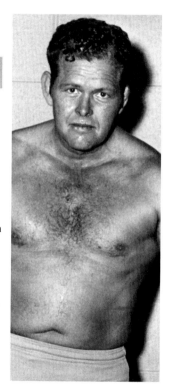

Fuller, who passed away in 1996, was part of a true wrestling family. His pop, Roy Welch, was a longtime Tennessee promoter with Nick Gulas from the 1940s-70s. Buddy's real name was Ed Welch and he was himself a wrestler and promoter from 1954-59 in the Gulf Coast region, which promoted in Alabama and Florida. Fuller later sold the territory to his cousin, Lee Fields, who was also a wrestler in the famed Fields Bros. tandems. Buddy Fuller's sons, Robert and Ron Fuller, wrestled and promoted in the Southeast region.

Fuller, Robert
(1960s-2000s)

The "Tennessee Studd" is the younger brother of former Tennessee promoter Ron Fuller. His entire family was involved in wrestling, mainly across the Southeast. Robert Fuller was almost exclusively a heel and he won many tag titles with his partner, Jimmy Golden. On screen, Fuller was a hoot, combining Southern wit with a cocky attitude. He later made appearances in Memphis, with his Studd's Stable, and WCW, managing Harlem Heat. [Col. Robert Parker]

Fuller, Ron
(1960s-1980s)

This longtime Knoxville-based wrestler was a noted promoter and businessman. His grandfather, Roy Welch, was a promoter, while his dad, Buddy Fuller, was a Southern grappler and promoter in Alabama and Florida. Ron Fuller co-promoted Southeastern Championship Wrestling during the 1970s and 1980s, which later changed its name to Continental.

Funk Jr., Dory
(1960s-1990s)

Scientific as they come, Dory Jr., the oldest son of Dory Funk Sr., had a prestigious career. He was an NWA world champion in 1969, having beaten Gene Kiniski for the title in Tampa, Fla. He also had a prolific career in Japan where he and his younger brother, Terry, were extremely popular draws for All-Japan in the 1970s and early 1980s. There were few, if any, territories he didn't appear in since the 1960s. Still active, he's a respected trainer in Florida. [Hoss Funk]

Dory Funk Jr.

Funk Sr., Dory
(1950s-1970s)

In Texas in the 1950s and 1960s, Dory Funk was king—king of the death matches. What you saw is what you got with Funk, as he lived the Texas ranch-hand gimmick he brought to the ring. Out of the Amarillo territory, Funk ran a longtime promotion, which was home to his sons, Terry and Dory Funk Jr. He died in 1973. [Texas Outlaw]

Dory Funk Sr. was always comfortable at home on the Double Cross Ranch.

Funk, Terry
(1960s-2000s)

This five-decade, road-weary traveler keeps going despite multiple injuries and false retirements. Funny thing is, he's still giving fans thrills. Terry's biggest days were the 1970s. He held the NWA world title for 14 months from 1975-77. He was also a legend in Japan where he and Dory Jr., his older brother, were immense crowd pleasers. He was still active into his 50s and setting new standards. Every time he retires, he returns even stronger and crazier. He helped put ECW and Japan's Frontier Martial Arts group on the map in the 1990s with his daredevil, hardcore performances. [Chainsaw Charlie]

Gagne, Greg
(1970s-1990s)

Being the boss' son did wonders for the career of Gagne, a second-generation technician. His pop, Verne, owned the AWA, where he saw most of his success. For most of the 1980s, he was an integral part of the promotion, teaming with Jim Brunzell as the popular High Flyers. The pair had a two-year reign as tag-team champions from 1981-83. When the AWA folded in 1990, he remained in wrestling as a backstage hand in WCW.

Gagne, Verne
(1950s-1980s)

One of the true legends, Verne was a college wrestling star at Minnesota, where he won the NCAA heavyweight title and parlayed that success in the pros. Gagne awarded himself the AWA title, a belt he'd hold nine times until 1980. In fairness, he took on challenges from every corner of the globe and as a stellar technician. His AWA was, at one time, one of the most successful promotions in the world. Virtually every major star walked through his turnstiles. In 1990, after financial difficulties and a changing wrestling climate, the AWA folded. But Gagne remains one of the most prominent fixtures in modern wrestling history.

Galento, Tony
(1930s-1950s)

A double-tough boxer who was often used as a special referee in the 1950s. Although his ring career was sometimes spent wrestling bears in special attractions, Galento, as a boxer, once fought Joe Louis for the heavyweight title.

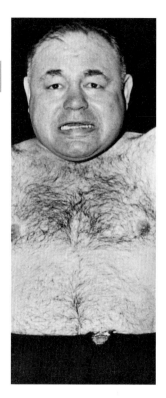

Garcia, Lillian
(1990s-2000s)

One of the WWF's few women announcers ever, Garcia began her career on "Monday Night Raw." Her career has also gotten her work singing the National Anthem at house shows, and even at professional baseball games.

Garea, Tony
(1960s-1980s)

The tall, lanky Italian has been one of the McMahon family's most loyal employees. He was a journeyman in East Coast rings, often in tag-team competition. From 1973-81, he held the company's tag title five times with partners Haystacks Calhoun, Dean Ho, Larry Zbyszko, and Rick Martel. He still works with the WWE as a road agent.

Garvin, Jimmy
(1970s-1990s)

The younger brother of Ron Garvin began his career as a teen-aged wrestling manager, guiding "brother" Terry Garvin and Bobby Shane. Garvin was seemingly everywhere during the cable explosion of the 1980s, traveling to Florida, World Class, and the NWA. Nicknamed "Handsome Jimmy," he was a quality mid-card attraction along with his wife and valet, Precious.

Garvin, Ronnie
(1970s-1990s)

Diminutive, yes; a pushover, no. Garvin portrayed a tough S.O.B. in the ring and often backed it up. Regionally, he was a solid star with adequate ring skills and fans always took to his small-town demeanor and fiery temper. His career reached the pinnacle in 1987 when he defeated Ric Flair for the NWA world title in Detroit. He finished his career with runs in the WWF and Smoky Mountain. [Rugged Ron; Hands of Stone]

Gaylord, Jeff
(1980s-1990s)

Once tabbed as a breakout star, Gaylord had trouble breaking out of the regional mindset. Often compared to the Ultimate Warrior due to his sculpted physique, Gaylord was popular in Memphis and Dallas, where he was promoted as a former football star from the University of Missouri. [The Hood]

Geigel, Bob
(1950s-1990s)

The Central States (Missouri, Kansas) promoter was a top grappler in the late 1950s and early 1960s, especially in tag competition. He was recognized as the AWA tag-team champion with Hard Boiled Haggerty after Gene Kiniski left H.B. without a partner. He also won belts with Otto Von Krupp. By the late 1960s, Geigel set his eyes on promoting the Central States region. For the next 10 years, he ran a fine territory. As the 1980s wound down, most territories were closing shop. Geigel ran one last super show with Giant Baba. It didn't draw well, but the Texan went down swinging.

George, Ed Don
(1930s-1950s)

A Native American wrestler who hearkens to the days when wrestling was considered a legit sport, George was an Olympic athlete and world wrestling champion. One of his matches, in 1934 against Jim McMillen, drew nearly 34,000 to Chicago's Wrigley Field. In 1928, he was an AAU and Olympic amateur wrestler. In 1930, he dethroned Gus Sonnenburg for the world title. That change was noteworthy because Sonnenburg, a famous football star, was beaten in a street fight. The NWA directors, not crazy about seeing their champ disgraced, gave the okay for George to win the title and restore the belt's credibility.

George, Mike
(1970s-1990s)

A veteran of the Kansas City, Mo., wars, the bruising George was a four-time Central States champion. He served as the Mid-South North American champion and often teamed with Bob Sweetan there. The stiff George once had an 83-minute draw with NWA world champion Ric Flair.

Giant Haystacks
(1960s-1990s)

One of England's top draws, the 6-11, bearded behemoth weighed nearly 500 pounds. He and Big Daddy, another UK attraction, drew thousands to matches in Wembley Arena in the 1980s. He died in 1998. [Loch Ness]

Gibson, Robert
(1980s-2000s)

Like his older brother, Ricky, Robert began his career as a referee in the Gulf Coast region before taking to the ring. Robert was a famous tag-team wrestler and part of perhaps the most popular tandem in history, the Rock & Roll Express. Less charismatic than his partner, Ricky Morton, Gibson was the perfect complement and held his own in the ring. Together, the pair toured most major promotions in the 1980s and were four-time NWA tag-team champions.

Gilbert, Doug
(1980s-2000s)

Son of former wrestler Tommy Gilbert and brother of Eddie, he was never far from his older bro in Memphis. He could wrestle if he chose, but he settled into a brawler's mold. He's a multi-time Southern tag-team champion who still shows up in the Southeast to wreak havoc. [Freddy Kreuger; Dark Patriot]

Gilbert, Eddie
(1970s-1980s)

When he wasn't contributing backstage, this second-generation star helped usher in the hardcore era in the ring. The son of Tommy Gilbert was a booker/scriptwriter for ECW, Memphis, Puerto Rico, and Windy City and Continental when he wasn't busy feuding with Jerry Lawler. In the ring, he was very productive. A great talker, he usually led stables of wrestlers called Hot Stuff Int. In Memphis, he called his group the Memphis Mafia and was involved in a famous angle in which he ran down Lawler with a car. Gilbert, in the prime of his career, died in his sleep in 1995 at age 33.

Gilberti, Glenn
(1990s-2000s)

How many have made a career of being a pest? Disco Glenn is one, that's for sure. Sporting a Honkytonk Man-type gimmick, the former WCW cruiserweight and tag-team champion is said to be a creative force behind the scenes for NWA-TNA. He once turned down a lucrative WWF offer to stay in WCW. [Disco Inferno; Disqo]

Gilzenberg, Willie
(1950s-1960s)

As a former promoter from Philadelphia, Gilzenberg was successful under the auspices of the NWA. But after having trouble getting the world champion to come to the Northeast, he and New York promoter, Vince McMahon Sr., partnered to form the WWWF in 1963. For that, he's remembered as an integral part of wrestling's history. He died in 1978.

Godfather, The
(1980s-2000s)

Another current-day wrestler with a multiple personality disorder, he began his career in the independents but quickly moved up the ladder due to his size and strength. In the WWF, he took on several gimmicks, like Papa Shango and Kama. But as the Godfather, he was a hit while wearing his patented pimp outfits. [Soul Taker; Papa Shango; Kama; Godfather; Goodfather]

Goldberg, Bill
(1990s-2000s)

This former college and pro football player was spotted by Lex Luger and Sting in a Georgia gym and urged to try wrestling. At first he was a cult favorite, but to everyone's surprise, his mainstream popularity skyrocketed in WCW, which culminated in a world title win over Hulk Hogan in his rookie campaign. Storylines claimed he had a 175-match win streak. Slowed by injuries, he debuted in the WWE in 2003 and has been searching for the magic that brought him success in WCW.

Gordienko, George
(1960s-1970s)

If he had his way, Gordienko probably would have been an artist. In addition to wrestling, he's been a respected painter and many of his works have been sold to collectors. Noted as a shooter in the ring, the Canadian-born wrestler was popular in Calgary where he won titles in the 1970s.

Gordy, Terry
(1970s-1990s)

Beginning his wrestling journey at the ripe age of 16, he defied his size and was seemingly destined to become a star. He was on the verge of quitting when he and Michael Hayes formed the Fabulous Freebirds with Buddy Roberts. His real success was realized in Japan where fans took to his realistic style that made them remember Bruiser Brody. By the late 1980s, his career was cruising. He won two Triple Crown titles in 1990 and in all was a seven-time All-Japan tag-team champion. He fought through a coma but was never the same and in 2001, he died. [The Executioner; Terry Mecca]

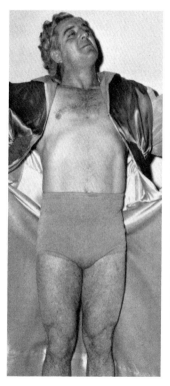

Gorgeous George
(1940s-1960s)

Born George Wagner of Seward, Neb., he was arguably the first must-see star in the history of pro wrestling. With the explosion of television wrestling in the early 1950s, Wagner's flamboyant act—complete with 24k gold hairpins—drew the nation's attention. The stars of today owe the "Human Orchid" a debt of thanks for helping the sport grow into a brand new form of entertainment.

Gotch, Frank
(1900-1910s)

Regarded as the best American wrestler ever, his legendary status is affirmed. The fact that even today's generation still talks about him is a testament to his celebrity. The Iowa native knew hundreds of holds and was the first American to earn the world's heavyweight title, which he won from Russian George Hackenschmidt in 1908 in Chicago. He died in 1917, in the prime of his life at age 41, from uremia.

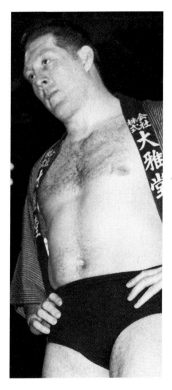

Gotch, Karl
(1950s-1980s)

This noted shooter was part of the Legionnaires tag team with Rene Goulet in the early 1970s. Born in Germany, he's still considered a legend in Japan. [Karl Krauser]

Goulet, Rene
(1960s-1980s)

As a lounge-singer lookalike, the French-Canadian was a fairly successful mid-level performer in the AWA where he toured in the 1960s. He made his way to the WWWF where he won the tag titles as the Legionnaires with Karl Gotch. He stayed with the WWF and has been working there as a road agent since retiring in the mid-1980s.

Grable, Joyce
(1950s-1970s)

Known as the "Golden Goddess," she took her nickname from film star Betty Grable. Her mom, Judy, wrestled, too.

Joyce Grable (left) shared the world tag team titles with Vicky Williams.

Grable, Judy
(1950s)

The mother of Joyce Grable, she toured the country extensively as one of the top names of the day. She also held a version of the women's belt in the 1950s.

Graham, Billy
(1960s-1980s)

Bodybuilding beach bum, Wayne Coleman, adopted the "Graham" name and carried it all the way to the WWWF world title in 1977. The "Superstar" was often a rule breaker but his flamboyant style made him a popular favorite almost everywhere he went. Graham, a known steroid user, was a major influence in wrestlers becoming physically impressive. Unfortunately, that drug use caused numerous health problems prior to his retirement in the late 1980s.

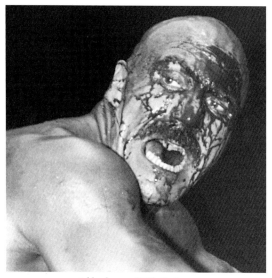

A blood-covered Billy Graham.

Graham, Eddie
(1940s-1980s)

Regarded by some as one of the greatest wrestlers of all time (certainly of the 1960s), Ed Gossett, a noted "brother" of Luke and Jerry Graham, was a Grade A main-event star and successful promoter in Florida. Like most Grahams in the ring, he was flamboyant and sported blond hair. With Jerry, he won three WWWF tag-team championships. When he settled on the business side, his group dominated the Sunshine State in the 1970s and 1980s. His territory was a cross-pollinated concoction on the NWA, AWA, and Mid-South. In the 1980s, Graham's promotion fell. Sadly, he committed suicide in 1985.

Graham, Jerry
(1950s-1970s)

The long-time partner of "brother" Eddie Graham, Jerry was the only real Graham among the famous tag team. He actually founded the famed team and frequently headlined at Madison Square Garden. Before his wrestling career, he was a World War II paratrooper. That belied his ring career where he was truly a villain. A great heel, he was an opponent of Buddy Rogers and Bruno Sammartino. The elder and "smarter" Graham, known as the "Dr.," was an average single's star but a superior tag-team wrestler. He held the WWWF tag title four times, including the very first crown awarded in 1957. He passed away in 1997.

Graham Sr., Luke
(1950s-1980s)

"Crazy" Luke was a wacky character in the WWWF and Southwest. Certainly not politically correct, his hijinks were a fun diversion. A tag-team champion with his "brother" Jerry, he ventured through California and Hawaii in the 1960s in addition to his time in the WWWF. Along with Tarzan Tyler, he was a former WWWF tag-team champion. The wild-haired heel also was found in the Central States where he held that company's single's title.

Graham, Mike
(1970s-2000s)

The Florida-based Graham was one of the premier junior heavyweights of the 1970s, primarily in the South. The son of Eddie Graham, he's a second-generation attraction who later joined WCW's booking team with Dusty Rhodes and Kevin Sullivan.

Grand Wizard, The
(1960s-1970s)

One of the quirkiest managers ever to round ringside, he was diminutive, wacky, and all fun. Wearing sunglasses and a turban, he took on a Middle Easterner gimmick while guiding many champions and miscreants in, among places, the WWWF, and is said to have been a favorite of the McMahon family. He passed away in 1983. [Abdullah Farouk]

Great Sasuke, The
(1980s-2000s)

A tremendous, masked, high-flyer from Japan who has been a constant on the independent scene. His career highlight was in the 1995 Super Juniors tournament. In May 2003, he was elected as a lawmaker in the local council chamber in Morioka, Japan. He has stuck to his wrestling roots by wearing his signature mask while in office.

Green, Sue
(1970s-1980s)

A journeyman ringster, she toured to limited success, but various reports have Green winning a version of the women's championship from Fabulous Moolah in 1976.

Guerrero Jr., Chavo
(1990s-2000s)

A third-generation start, the son of Chavo Guerrero is a cruiserweight who has appeared in WCW and WWF. He struggled to find his own identity, but persevered to win the WCW cruiserweight title. Of late, he's been an important member of the WWE family, winning the tag-team titles with his uncle, Eddy Guerrero. [Lt. Loco]

Guerrero Sr., Chavo
(1970s-1980s)

The eldest son of Gory Guerrero, he was a former Texas champion and popular among Latino fans in U.S. border towns. Like all the Guerreros, he was a talented high flyer and had success in the Mid-South territory. He also teamed with his brothers, Hector, Mando, and Eddy.

Guerrero, Eddy
(1980s-2000s)

A talented high flyer and member of the legendary family (he's Chavo Jr.'s uncle), Eddy's career began to take flight in Mexico where he teamed with Art Barr to wild success in the early 1990s. He also wrestled in Japan but was brought to the U.S. by ECW in the mid-90s. Despite having to recover from a horrific car accident, he has restarted his career in WWE, where he's won the Intercontinental and tag-team titles and is consistently one of the best performers in the world. [Latino Heat; Black Tiger; Mascara Magica]

Guerrero, Hector
(1970s-1980s)

An acrobatic Latino star, the son of Gory Guerrero wrestled mainly in the Southeast. The tallest of the wrestling Guerreros, he brought many Lucha Libre skills, which, at the time, were very new to American fans. He won regional titles and also had a run in the NWA in the junior heavyweight division as Lazor Tron. [Lazor Tron; Gobbledy Gooker]

Gunkel, Ray
(1960s-1970s)

A clean-cut and dashing baby-face wrestler-promoter in Georgia, he died in 1972 from injuries suffered in a match earlier one evening against Ox Baker in Savannah, Ga. Baker, known for his heart punch move, administered the move on Gunkel and he inadvertently bruised Gunkel's heart. The injury was reportedly the cause of his death. He was also a noted promoter of wrestling in Georgia and, when he died, his wife, Ann, took over until the promotion closed in 1974.

Gunn, Bart
(1990s-2000s)

Formerly one-half of the Smoking Gunns tag team with Billy Gunn, he was a cowboy character in the WWF after a brief stint on the Florida independent circuit. With Billy, the twosome won three tag-team titles. Bart ventured on his own, winning the "Brawl for All" contest and appeared poised for a UFC career before he was kayoed by Butterbean at Wrestlemania 15. Ever since, he's been in All-Japan trying to escape that embarrassment. [Mike Barton; Bodacious Bart]

Gunn, Billy
(1990s-2000s)

Perhaps no current-day wrestler has been in the right place at the right time more often than Gunn, an average mid-carder who found success in the WWF as one member of Degeneration X after playing a cowboy gimmick with Bart Gunn. Together, they won three tag-team titles. Billy later joined with Road Dogg in DX and claimed five more tag-team titles. He's also a former Intercontinental champion. [B.A.; Bad Ass Billy Gunn; Mr. Ass]

Hackenschmidt, George
(1900-1910s)

Recognized in 1904 as the first world champion in the line of NWA title holders, he earned that recognition after a match with then-North American champion, Tom Jenkins, in New York City. With a chiseled physique, he looked like a dominant force. After dodging American hopeful Frank Gotch for several years, Hackenschmidt was dethroned in a Chicago match in 1908.

Haku
(1980s-2000s)

Like a cat with nine lives, Haku has been reincarnated many times in many territories with various gimmicks. He's been everything from a king to a warrior, but this legendary tough guy is multi-talented. The kick-boxer and martial artist has wrestled in New Zealand, Canada, Australia, Singapore, Canada, and all over the U.S. Not known to hold many titles in his career, he has won the WWF tag belts (with Andre the Giant) and WCW hardcore belt. [Meng; King Tonga; Tonga Warrior; King Haku]

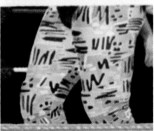

Hall, Scott
(1980s-2000s)

Known mostly for his blockbuster role in the New World Order with Kevin Nash and Hulk Hogan, Hall was originally a territory star from the early 1980s Florida scene. After trips to the AWA (where he was tag-team champion with Curt Hennig) and WCW, he received a new look in the WWF as Razor Ramon. He had a brief run as Intercontinental champion, but the company cut him and Nash loose in 1995. He then went to WCW where he was part of the hot NWO gimmick, which drew capacity crowds for nearly two years. Unfortunately, his personal demons derailed his career. [Gator Scott Hall; Razor Ramon]

Hansen, Stan
(1970s-2000s)

A true Texas legend, he is known for being one of the most rugged wrestlers ever and many would-be opponents have run from him in the ring. But his true success came in Japan where he has been a two-decade attraction on the singles and tag-team scene. His list of accomplishments include four All-Japan Triple Crown titles from 1990-95, eight All-Japan tag-team titles, and the AWA world title in 1985.

Hanson, Swede
(1950s-1980s)

Teamed up with Rip Hawk, Hanson was a feared tag-team wrestler in the Carolinas. He was a husky heel who exhibited great chemistry with Hawk, with whom he was a multiple tag-team champion. Hanson passed away in 2002 at age 68.

Harlem Heat
(1990s)

Ray and Booker Huffman began their careers in the Texas independents before getting a call from WCW in the early 1990s. At first they were heels, but there was no denying their popularity. Together, the duo won the world tag titles 10 times.

Hart Foundation, The
(1980s-1990s)

Bret Hart and Jim
Niedhart, managed by Jimmy
Hart, made up this tag team
in the WWF's early-1980s
era. Brokered to the WWF
from Calgary Stampede, they
blended perfectly as Niedhart
provided the power while
Hart provided the technical
skills. In the beginning, they
were glorified mid-carders
but eventually caught the
attention of Vince McMahon
Jr. Their feuds with the
Rockers and British Bulldogs
showcased four-star matches
nightly. The Foundation
won two WWF tag-team
championships, in 1987 and
1990.

Hart, Bret
(1980s-2000s)

Bret blended a distinct style that combined Japanese, American, and Mexican styles and was key in bringing wrestling into a new era with his creative flair for moves and strong work ethic. In Calgary, he was a five-time Stampede North American champion. In the U.S., he became a WWF icon, winning the world belt five times from 1992-97 and the Intercontinental title twice, from 1991-92. He broke ties with the McMahon family on ugly terms. He ventured to WCW where he was a two-time world champ in 1999. He was forced to retire from post-concussion syndrome, stroke, and stress from his brother Owen's 1999 death.

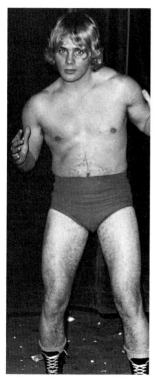

Hart, Bruce
(1970s-2000s)

Extremely intelligent wrestler who is credited with bringing the Japanese style to North America. In the Hart family, Bruce has been the mastermind behind the scenes. He helped his father, Stu, operate Calgary Stampede's training center for many years. In addition, he held the Stampede British Commonwealth belt five times. In the late 1980s, he trained and teamed with Brian Pillman. Bruce remains active with hopes of a Calgary revival.

Hart, Gary
(1970s-1990s)

This ex-wrestler reached stardom as a manager in Florida, Dallas, and the NWA. He has had classic feuds with Dusty Rhodes in which he managed foes like Kabuki and the Great Muta against Rhodes and a host of heroes.

Hart, Jimmy
(1980s-2000s)

Hart was a famous heel manager who started in Memphis with the help of Jerry Lawler. His best years were in the early 1980s, when he was at the center of the Lawler-Andy Kaufman feud. He went on to the WWF, and later WCW, where he managed multiple tag-team and single's champions. Before wrestling, he was a singer in the band, the Gentrys. He still has his hands in the business as a promoter.

Hart, Keith
(1970s-1980s)

One of the lesser-known Hart family members, Keith was popular in Canada, Hawaii, and England. He won numerous belts, including the Calgary Mid-Heavyweight and tag-team titles (with brother Bruce). He was considered too small for a major market but, just like all the Harts, he was a technically sound grappler.

Hart, Owen
(1980s-1990s)

A special performer of the modern era, he died tragically at age 34 performing a stunt in 1999. Owen, the baby of the Calgary Hart family, was a high flyer in Canada and Japan, who was destined to become a star. He wanted to be an Olympic wrestler, but the pro ranks always called him. In Calgary, he teamed with brother, Bruce, and held the Calgary Stampede title in feuds with Makhan Singh. Sometimes deemed too small, he broke into the WWF twice as the Blue Blazer. When he finally had a chance to be himself, Owen shined, winning the WWF Intercontinental title, European title, and tag titles three times.

Hart, Stu
(1940s-1980s)

He's the man who started it all for the Hart clan. A former amateur standout, he turned pro in the 1940s and his imprint is still felt today. His family run promotion, Calgary Stampede, has, since 1948, been the home of pioneers, rebels, and miscreants. Many graduated from his training to become some of wrestling's biggest stars. Only the toughest of the tough survived training in his dreaded dungeon. Alums? How about Davey Boy Smith, Dynamite Kid, Bad News Brown, not to mention his all-star roll call of sons. Many Japanese stars have also passed through his mitts. In 1986, he stepped into the ring for the last time at age 70.

Hashimoto, Shinya
(1980s-2000s)

The bulky, Japanese star has been on top since the mid-1980s. Aligned with Keiji Mutoh and Masahiro Chono, he was part of the country's strong style and was arguably the nation's top draw in the 1990s. His accolades include the IWGP title three times from 1993-96 and the NWA world title in 2001.

Hawk
(1980s-2000s)

Not particularly talented in the ring, Hawk had one thing going for him that made him a sure thing: a gimmick. As one half of the Road Warriors, Hawk (born Mike Hegstrand) had loads of charisma when he burst on the scene in the early 1980s with his partner, Animal. Perhaps the hottest tag-team creation ever, the Road Warriors were in high demand for much of the 1980s and helped usher in a new era of big men. In 2003, Hawk lost his life.

Hayes, Michael
(1970s-2000s)

One of the greatest interviews in wrestling history, Hayes can make you laugh, cry, and scream all in one interview. As the famed leader of the Fabulous Freebirds, he was a main-event star wherever he went through the 1980s. Some of his exploits took place in World Class, Georgia Championship, and the Mid-South region. Along with Terry Gordy and Buddy Roberts, they were genuine heat seekers and are fondly remembered. [Dok Hendrix]

Haynes, Billy Jack
(1970s-1990s)

The well-chiseled Haynes traveled to Florida and the Central States but he rose to the top in Portland. With his regional days behind him, he took an offer to wrestle in the WWF in the early 1980s. It proved to be a mistake. Despite a Wrestlemania III match against Ken Patera, he never caught on. After that tour, he began promoting in Oregon, where he has been ever since. [Black Blood]

Headbangers, The
(1990s)

Chaz Warrington (Mosh) and Glen Ruth (Thrash) were East Coast independent stars when they turned a stint in Smoky Mountain Wrestling into a WWF contract. Riding high, using a grunge-rock gimmick, they held the WWF tag titles for a month in 1997. [Flying Nuns; The Spiders (Mosaic and Tarantula)]

Chaz Warrington

Headhunters, The
(1980s-2000s)

Are they twin sons of Abdullah the Butcher? They sure look it. Manuel and Victor Santiago sure were a sight to see. Who could forget 400-pound men flying off the top rope? They rode their gimmick to titles in Japan and Mexico. With the exception of a tiny stint in the WWF managed by Jim Cornette, U.S. stardom eluded them.

Heavenly Bodies, The
(1990s)

When Jim Cornette opened Smoky Mountain Wrestling in the early 1990s, he needed a tag-team in the mold of the Midnight Express. The Bodies, comprised of former Express member Stan Lane and newbie Tom Pritchard, picked up the slack. Later, when Lane quit, Jimmy Del Ray was brought in. They didn't make people forget about the Midnights, but for a regional throwback team, they fit the bill.

Heenan, Bobby
(1960s-1990s)

Few men in wrestling have had the access to their wit as Bobby Heenan, the finest manager to ever live. Heenan began his career as a wrestler in Indiana but used his wit and interview ability to build up stables of wrestlers. In the AWA and WWF, he was an all-purpose show stopper and behind-the-scenes genius. He helped lead the careers of Blackjack Lanza, Nick Bockwinkel, Curt Hennig, and Rick Rude and has had a career-long, onscreen feud against Hulk Hogan that culminated in Hogan's Wrestlemania III match against Andre the Giant at the Pontiac Silver Dome.

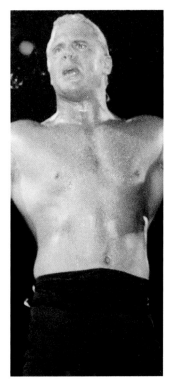

Hennig, Curt
(1970s-2000s)

Considered to be the perfect athlete while with the WWF in the 1990s, he was the son of Larry Hennig. Curt won the AWA world title in 1987 and later grabbed the WWF I-C belt. One of the best workers in his heyday, he was known as a prankster backstage. Hennig lost his life in 2003. [Mr. Perfect]

Heyman, Paul
(1980s-2000s)

What else can be said of Heyman. He's been a jack-of-all-trades in wrestling, going from fan, photographer, and manager to booker, commentator, television director, and creative genius. He ventured to many promotions, including Memphis, the AWA and NWA. After his ECW group closed its doors in 2001, he settled into an on-again, off-again role with the WWE, managing Brock Lesnar and Big Show. [Paul E. Dangerously]

Hogan, Hulk
(1970s-2000s)

A true superstar, few can argue he made the biggest impact on wrestling. As a television personality, he captured the attention of fans globally in the early 1980s, which enabled the WWF to rule the roost. He was a 12-time world champion in WWF and WCW (six times in each promotion). Many fans got their start in wrestling from watching Hogan. [Terry Boulder; Hulk Machine; Hollywood Hogan; Mr. America]

Hulk Hogan flexes some muscle.

Holly, Crash
(1990s-2000s)

This West Coast independent wrestler, despite his small frame, reached fame in the WWF as Bob Holly's "cousin." At 5-6, it would seem the deck is stacked against him, but he found a niche as a hardcore/comedy act. He won the WWF hardcore belt a record 13 times. He's also a former European and tag-team champion with Bob. He died in 2003. [Erin O'Grady]

Holly, Molly
(1990s-2000s)

In an era when women's wrestling is often a joke, the short sweetheart has tried to bring some respectability to the division. A native of Minnesota, she trained in Florida. She used her connections with Randy Savage as a springboard to WCW in the late 1990s. From there, she hit the WWF and has been a staple ever since, even winning the women's title. [Miss Madness]

Hollywood Blondes, The
(1970s-1990s)

The name of several tag teams of the past, one of the originals were Buddy Roberts and Jerry Brown. Even Steve Austin and Brian Pillman called themselves the Blondes in WCW in the early 1990s. In Memphis, Ken Timbs and Dusty Wolfe used the name. In Puerto Rico, Larry Sharpe and Jack Evans used the Blondes gimmick.

Honkytonk Man, The
(1980s-2000s)

Wayne Ferris is a Memphis-area legend, who borrowed from Elvis Presley's image to create this gimmick. Wrestling is in his family. His cousins are wrestlers Jerry Lawler and Carl Fergie. [The Moondog]

Horner, Tim
(1980s-1990s)

A talented light heavyweight, his smallish size prevented him from reaching true stardom. Even so, Horner made a nice career in the UWF and NWA in the early 1980s, teaming with Brad Armstrong. He always had decent runs, but the main event was elusive although he was a multi-time regional champion. Later on, he also was Jim Cornette's business partner in Smoky Mountain.

Humperdink, Oliver
(1970s-1990s)

Red Sutton was a journeyman wrestler in the Mid-Atlantic (where he held the TV title) and Central States area, but found his calling as a manager in Florida, WCW, and the WWF (where he guided Bam Bam Bigelow) in the 1980s. A career nemesis of Dusty Rhodes, Humperdink always had a beefy stable to call on to do his dirty deeds. [Sir Oliver Humperdink; Big Daddy Dink]

Hurricane, The
(1990s-2000s)

Super heroes come in all sizes, right? Hurricane may be small, but he's large on talent. After breaking into wrestling in the Carolina independents with Shannon Moore, Shane Helms caught on in the WCW cruiserweight division. There, he teamed with Moore and Evan Karagis. When he finally got to the WWE, he was anointed with the Hurricane gimmick, based loosely around his interest in comic book characters. With a marketable name, Helms has settled into his popular cruiserweight role. [Shane Helms; Sugar Sean]

Iaukea, Curtis
(1950s-1990s)

Once considered a hardcore legend, Iaukea was an odd-looking character with a scarred bald head. He won numerous regional belts while tearing up foes in Hawaii, Australia, and the WWF. Also, he is said to have influenced Bruiser Brody. [King Curtis; Master]

Inoki, Antonio
(1970s-2000s)

Like his one-time friend and partner, the late Giant Baba, Inoki reached legendary status in Japan. After training under Rikidozan, Inoki quickly became a star and retained his success all the way to his retirement in the 1990s.

Iron Sheik, The
(1970s-2000s)

Born Kosrow Vaziri, this former WWF world champion is said to have been a bodyguard for the Shah of Iran. He had a background in weightlifting and he used his power in wrestling. After hitting many areas around the country, he settled in as a controversial figure in the WWF in the 1980s. In December 1983, he surprisingly beat Bob Backlund for the title in New York only to lose it a week later to Hulk Hogan. [Great Hossein; Col. Mustafa]

Jacqueline
(1980s-2000s)

The spunky spitfire, trained in Texas under Skandor Akbar, made her debut in 1989. Since then, she's been to WCW, the WWE as a valet and manager, and the USWA, where she won a record 14 women's titles from 1993-96. [Sweet Georgia Brown; Jackie; Miss Texas]

Jannetty, Marty
(1980s-1990s)

Known as a high-flying technical star, the Kansas-based Jannetty began in Bob Geigel's Central States group. Too small to be a heavyweight, he teamed with Shawn Michaels. Capitalizing on the MTV generation, the duo, named the Midnight Rockers, blitzed the AWA and won the world tag titles. Later, the duo maxed their potential in the WWF as the Rockers. With Michaels seen as the next superstar, Jannetty, not to be outdone, relaunched his singles career and even won the WWF Intercontinental title in 1993.

Jarrett, Jeff
(1980s-2000s)

A second generation star from Memphis, Jeff started his career in his teens. Initially he looked like a beanpole, but through hard work, he matured into a top U.S. star. He has always fought the label of being too "regional" looking, but defied the critics and served time as the WWF Intercontinental and tag-team champion. In 2000, he won the WCW world title from Dallas Page in Chicago. Of late, he's been trying to revitalize the NWA-TNA promotion based in Nashville. [Double J]

Jarrett, Jerry
(1960s-2000s)

Long considered a wrestling genius, Jarrett has been an astute businessman in the Memphis region. He was a better-than-average wrestler in the 1970s, but found his true calling as promoter of Memphis wrestling. Alongside Jerry Lawler, the territory survived most changes in the business and was, for a time, considered a time-warp promotion. By the 1990s, Jarrett had sold off the group and left wrestling altogether, but resurfaced in 2002 as the owner of NWA-TNA. He's hopeful he has some old magic left to make the new group a success.

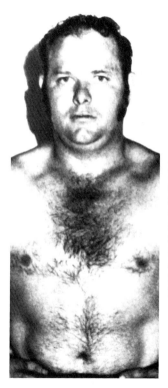

Jay, Kenny
(1960s-2000s)

The "Sodbuster" was a legendary jobber in the Midwest in the 1960s and 1970s. In his heyday, he held surprising victories over Harley Race and Bobby Heenan, both of which made him famous with fans. His career high was wrestling Muhammad Ali in an exhibition match in Chicago as Ali geared up for his match with Antonio Inoki. Well into his 60s, Jay still wrestled on independent cards.

Jazz
(1990s-2000s)

Probably as tough as any women's wrestler, she started her career in 1999 as Justin Credible's manager in ECW. But Jazz sought higher ground and continued to train for wrestling. That diligence paid off: in 2003, she became the WWE champ. [A.C. Jazz]

Johnson, Rocky
(1960s-1980s)

The "Soulman" may be best known as the Rock's pop, but he was a top drawing wrestler the world over. He had strong ties to boxing and had an Ali-like foot shuffle. Promoters hoped to cash in on his African-American Superman look, and he and Tony Atlas once held the WWWF tag belts in 1983.

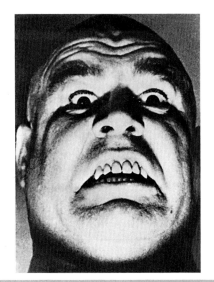

Johnson, Tor
(1930s-1960s)

As freaky looking as they come, this balding menace wrestled as the Swedish Angel in many territories. He even parlayed his looks into a spot in the Ed Wood cult classic, "Plan 9 From Outer Space." He also had bit parts in more than 25 films, including ones starring Abbott & Costello and Bela Lugosi. [Swedish Angel]

Jumping Bomb Angels
(1980s)

Following the success of Japan's Crush Gals, All-Japan Women's promoters promoted Noriyo Tateno and Itsuki Yamazaki as the Angels to mega-stardom. They were even victorious in a brief stateside stint in the WWF in 1988, winning the now-defunct women's tag-team titles from the Glamour Girls.

Junkyard Dog, The
(1970s-1990s)

After hitting most regions of the country, Sylvester Ritter was the biggest star in Mid-South in the early 1980s. As an African American, he had a loyal following in New Orleans. Riotous crowds watched him in explosive feuds against Ted DiBiase and Butch Reed. While there, he won the Mid-South title four times. Later on, he traveled to the WWF and helped take the group national. His career over, he died in 1998 from injuries suffered in a car wreck. [Big Daddy Ritter; Stagger Lee]

Kabuki
(1970s-1980s)

One of manager Gary Hart's assassins from Florida to battle Dusty Rhodes, Kabuki was shrouded in mystery. He spewed green mist at his opponents and also during his pre-match ritual. As a wrestler, Kabuki was talented and appeared in other U.S. territories like World Class.

Kai, Lelani
(1970s-1980s)

This journeyman wrestler, along with Judy Martin, formed the Glamour Girls in the WWF during the 1980s

Kamala
(1970s-2000s)

James Harris was a territory journeyman who had one thing going for him: his size. The 350-pounder adopted the Ugandan headhunter gimmick and gave his career life. He's often been a main event monster in Memphis, World Class, and the WWF. [Bad News Harris]

Kane
(1980s-2000s)

Glenn Osborne has been an underrated performer in the WWF, but his time on a national level shows his uniqueness to the company. After several failed gimmicks, he went to the minors to learn. By the late 1990s, he was back in the WWE as Kane, Undertaker's "brother." A former world singles and tag-team champion, he's been one of the better big men in recent memory. [Fake Diesel; Unibomb; Isaac Yankem; X-Mas Creature]

Keirn, Steve
(1970s-2000s)

The Floridian reached wide appeal as the Fabulous Ones with Stan Lane in the early 1980s. The team, managed by Jackie Fargo, was a spin-off of the popular 1960s team, the Fabulous Fargos. Keirn, always a solid presence in the ring, was a fine single's performer with runs in Florida and the WWF. [Skinner]

Kelly, Kevin
(1980s-1990s)

Kelly, a former bodybuilding pal of Hulk Hogan's, was a bleached-blond, big-talker who could back it up. After touring World Class, AWA, and Windy City, he caught on briefly in the WWF as Nailz. After his career, he became a real-life bounty collector. [Mr. Magnificent; The Convict; Nailz]

Kid Kash
(1990s-2000s)

Introduced to wrestling by Ricky Morton, this Kid Rock look-alike wrestled in the Southeast for many years before getting a break in ECW. A spectacular high flyer, he's also been an integral part of NWA-TNA, winning the X-Division title. [Dave Cash; David Taylor; David Morton]

Kidman, Billy
(1990s-2000s)

Trained by the Wild
Samoans in Allentown, Pa.,
this acrobatic star became
a cult hit in WCW first as a
member of Raven's Flock.
He's tried hard to reach
beyond the cruiserweight
level (he even feuded with
Hulk Hogan), but his
true calling is wrestling
against other flyers like Rey
Mysterio Jr. and Juventud
Guerrera. To his credit, he's
a former WWE and WCW
cruiserweight champion.
[Kid Flash; Kidman]

Killer Khan
(1960s-1980s)

Khan was a career-long villain with a wild-eyed gimmick. A premier brawler in his day, he was a top draw around the country and had several high profile feuds in the WWF with Andre the Giant and Hulk Hogan. Later, in World Class, he had bloodbaths with the Missing Link and Terry Gordy.

Killings, Ron
(1990s-2000s)

An energetic wrestler with quick striking moves, Killings began in Memphis, but quickly hit the WWF as a rapping performer. After a stint as Jesse James' partner, he took off for the NWA. He won that belt in 2002 and has been called the first-ever black NWA world champion. [K-Krush; K-Kwik]

King, Sonny
(1960s-1970s)

Although he never set out to be a champion of civil rights, he is recognized as the first African American to hold a major belt. In 1972, he and Jay Strongbow defeated Baron Scicluna and King Curtis for the WWWF tag-team titles. He later ventured to Georgia, where he adopted the Isaac Hayes look and became a manager.

Kiniski, Gene
(1950s-1970s)

Generally considered one of the more accomplished wrestlers in history. In 1966, he shocked the world by beating Lou Thesz in St. Louis for the NWA world title which he held for three years. He was also an AWA world champion. He was rough and smug in the ring, a style enjoyed by his Japanese fans. His legendary status leaves some to believe he was one of the top 10 greats of all time. He left a family legacy as well, with his wrestling sons Nick and Kelly Kiniski.

Knobbs, Brian
(1980s-2000s)

Formerly of the Nasty Boys tag team, Knobbs never professed to be a great wrestler. Doesn't matter. His fun, brawling gimmick was good enough to give him a career. He's a former AWA and WWF tag-team champ, as well as a former WCW hardcore champion.

Koloff, Ivan
(1960s-1990s)

One of the few Russian-born wrestlers, he was feared but also admired for his skills. He held the NWA tag title four times, but his shining moment came in 1971 while winning the WWF world championship from Bruno Sammartino, which ended Bruno's eight-year reign. Despite the win, Koloff only held the belt for 21 days before dropping it to Pedro Morales.

Koloff, Nikita
(1980s-1990s)

Wrestled as a Russian but he was really from the Midwest. He was a very stiff competitor, but a tremendous heel. In the NWA Mid-Atlantic area, he won tag titles and singles titles teaming with Ivan Koloff. He reached superstar status when he turned baby face and teamed with Dusty Rhodes. These days, he owns a franchise of gyms in the Mid-Atlantic area.

Konnan
(1980s-2000s)

Discovered in San Diego where he was a Navy man, he was a huge hit in every major Mexican promotion in the 1990s before getting a spot in WCW. In 1993, his match with Cien Caras drew nearly 50,000 in Mexico City. Has held the AAA and EMLL world titles, as well as WCW tag and U.S. title. [El Centurion; Max Moon]

La Parka
(1980s-2000s)

This very entertaining Mexican star with a skeleton outfit made a name for himself in WCW with his flair for throwing chairs. He remains a star in Lucha Libre.

Ladd, Ernie
(1960s-1980s)

An extremely influential African-American wrestler who was prominent in the NFL before crossing over to wrestling. At 6'7, the Big Cat was a huge presence. He toured the world winning numerous regional titles, particularly throughout the Mid-South and Georgia.

Landel, Buddy
(1980s-2000s)

Destined for stardom, bad luck and poor timing were Landel's biggest foes. This pure Southern performer used his Nature Boy gimmick well. In 1985, when Ric Flair needed time off, promoters were set to give the NWA belt to Landel, but he no-showed. Later, he honorably battled back from drug abuse and was offered a gig in the WWF, but he injured himself before the match and was never seen again. That's wrestling's loss, since he was a great talker and entertaining performer wherever he went.

Lane, Stan
(1980s-2000s)

Lane, with a dashing, made-for-television look, has been a fine tag-team wrestler. Trained by Ric Flair, he was one-half of two very successful teams, the Fabulous Ones (with Steve Keirn) and the Midnight Express (with Bobby Eaton). With those teams, he was a Southern and NWA world tag-team champion. Lane also found regional success with Tom Pritchard as the Heavenly Bodies in Smoky Mountain Wrestling.

Lawler, Brian
(1980s-2000s)

The real-life son of Jerry Lawler, he has his pop's gift for interviews and has been a fun heel wrestler. He began as a light heavyweight jobber in Memphis, but quickly rose through the ranks thanks to his dad's influence. In fairness, he was worth promoting. He had numerous main event feuds in Memphis, even a few against his dad. By the late 1990s, he finally got a chance in the WWF. Teamed with Scott Taylor as Too Cool, the duo electrified crowds with big moves and break dancing. They also won the tag-team titles in 2000. [Brian Christopher; Grandmaster Sexay; New Kid Brian]

Lawler, Jerry
(1970s-2000s)

Few wrestlers have had as many opponents as the King. He holds wins over Hulk Hogan, the Rock, Steve Austin, and just about every contemporary wrestler. For most of his career, he has been a part owner of various wrestling companies based in Memphis and has held the Southern Heavyweight title more than anyone. He has wrestled relentlessly since the 1970s and has survived many industry changes. Lawler is also an artist, a former disc jockey, would-be politician, talk show host, color commentator, and singer. Lawler's influence is still felt as a broadcaster. His sons, Brian and Kevin, both have had wrestling careers. [The King]

Legionaires, The
(1970s)

Sgt. Jacques Goulet led this team with various partners winning both the WWWF and WWA tag titles. Sometimes he used partner Karl Gotch, a known shooter, in the WWWF and other times Goulet used soldier Zarinoff Le Beouf.

LeRoux, Lash
(1990s-2000s)

Louisiana-born, this redhead climbed the ladder in WCW, going from the Power Plant to cruiserweight hero in short time. He also held the WCW tag titles with Chavo Guerrero. [Cpl. Cajun]

Lesnar, Brock
(1990s-2000s)

Even as a college wrestler at Minnesota, Lesnar seemed destined for the pro ranks. After winning the NCAA heavyweight title, he signed a WWE contract. Built like a truck, Lesnar is power personified. Combined with his amateur background, he's a new-age force. Shortly after his debut, he beat the Rock, winning his first of what should be many world titles.

Lewin, Mark
(1950s-1980s)

Longevity has been the word for this strongman who began his career in the 1950s. He toured around the globe, from New Zealand and England to Japan, Canada, and the U.S. From 1978-80, "Maniac Mark" was a five-time Brass Knux champ and his feuds with the Sheik in Detroit are classics. His brothers, Ted and Donn, also wrestled.

A younger Mark Lewin.

Liger, Jushin
(1980s-2000s)

Like Tiger Mask before him, this Japanese star got his gimmick from a cartoon spin-off. Before becoming a star in Japan, he wowed fans in Mexico and Canada. In New Japan, he was an 11-time junior heavyweight champ and had classic matches with Chris Benoit, Owen Hart, and Ultimo Dragon. He wrestled briefly in the U.S., winning the WCW cruiserweight title. Though his success came a world away, for much of the 1990s, he was arguably the best on the planet.

Lita
(1990s-2000s)

Amy Dumas trained with the Hardy Boys and found herself as a valet in ECW before hitting the road in WWE, where she set new heights for women wrestlers. The former women's champ is also the girlfriend of Matt Hardy. [Miss Congeniality]

Londos, Jim
(1930s-1950s)

The name "Golden Greek" surely fit Londos, as he looked like a Greek god. He was said to have been introduced to wrestling through the circus, where he was an acrobat. Regarded as one of the best of his day, he held two versions of the world title (1934 and 1950) and was a big hit on the East Coast, where he was a frequent opponent of Ed "Strangler" Lewis.

Lord Littlebrook
(1950s-1980s)

This Brit is arguably the greatest midget wrestler of all time. He used a nobleman gimmick and claims to be the first to do a somersault off the top rope. He often held the midget world title and feuded with Sky Low Low and Little Beaver.

Louis, Joe
(1950s-1960s)

Remembered as a legendary boxer, he's only one of three former pro boxing champs to get into wrestling. Louis won the hearts of Americans with a victory over German Max Schmeling. During World War II, Louis enlisted in the military where he boxed some exhibition fights for the troops. In all, he defended his world boxing title 25 times, but because of severe tax debt, he was forced to make some easy money in wrestling and appeared as a special attraction, both as a wrestler and referee in Detroit, among other areas.

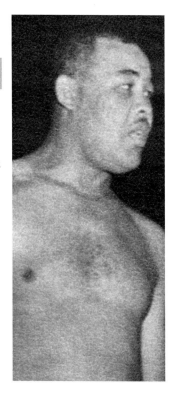

Low-Ki
(1990s-2000s)

The Brooklyn-born shooter combines Lucha Libre, martial arts, and traditional wrestling into a compact package. He has been to many regional groups and frequents Japan's Zero-One, too. He's won numerous independent belts.

Luger, Lex
(1980s-1990s)

This muscled Florida
native was pegged to be
the next superstar after
a Sunshine State tour.
He indeed became WCW
world champ in 1991,
but his days on top were
average. He was a high
profile employee for 10
years in WCW and WWF.
After a long buildup to
win the WWF belt, he
was sent packing. He
had decent matches
with Sting and Ric Flair.
Before wrestling, he was
a football player at Penn
State. [Total Package;
Narcissist]

Lynn, Jerry
(1990s-2000s)

This technically sound athlete is capable of any style around the world. Cast aside for most of his career because of his size, his talent was finally recognized when he had memorable feuds with Rob Van Dam and Justin Credible, and beat Credible for the ECW world title in 2000. The WWE saw some of his potential and gave him a shot as the lightweight champion in 2001, but that stint was short. Today, Lynn remains a viable talent on the independent scene and in NWA-TNA. [Mr. J.L]

Maeda, Akira
(1970s-1990s)

One of the sport's legit tough guys, he was trained by Karl Gotch. Displeased with American-style wrestling, he started the shoot-fighting group UWF in 1988 under the premise its matches were "real." The group started a revolution in the sport, continued with promotions like UFC and Pride. In the pro style, he had a distinct realness about him that drew many new fans to the sport. [Kwik Kick Lee]

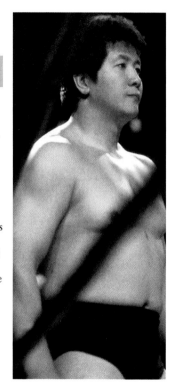

Magnum T.A.
(1970s-1980s)

Also known by his real name, Terry Allen, this handsome wrestler was a Tom Selleck look-alike whose career was cut short due to paralysis from a car wreck. Most fans still remember his tearful comeback in the early 1990s as an announcer. As a wrestler, Allen was popular in Florida, the NWA, and Mid-Atlantic territories where he often teamed with his pal, Dusty Rhodes. He had a good look and was adept in the ring, winning the U.S. title two times in 1985.

Mahoney, Balls
(1980s-2000s)

After meager beginnings in Smoky Mountain, this native New Jersey brawler patterned his career after Cactus Jack. He's been slammed on fire, thumb tacks, and tables in ECW and continues to work in Puerto Rico and East Coast independents. In ECW, he was a three-time tag-team champion. [Abbudah Singh; Boo Bradley]

Maivia, Peter
(1960s-1980s)

A real-life Hawaiian chieftain who brought fame to the island as a main event star the world over, he was heavily tattooed, as are all tribal leaders, and very muscular with a million dollar smile. In the ring, he was a fun performer who, in addition to wrestling in Hawaii, was always at home in New York for the WWWF. The father-in-law of Rocky Johnson. He also promoted Polynesian Pro in Honolulu from 1980-82 before he died in 1982 from cancer.

Malenko, Boris
(1950s-1990s)

Larry Simon was a superb technical wrestler and trainer. Considered the originator of the Russian chain match, he was never shy by a microphone. His illustrious career took him all over the world, including Japan, where he was treated like a demigod in his matches with Antonio Inoki. His sons Joe and Dean had fine careers themselves. Later in his career, he became a trainer in Florida, producing talent like X-Pac and Norman Smiley.

Malenko, Dean
(1980s-2000s)

A master of submission and counter holds, the son of Boris Malenko was just as tough in real life as his TV persona. Although he had great matches in Japan, the former WCW cruiserweight champ also had five-star bouts in ECW with Chris Benoit and Eddy Guerrero.

Malice
(1990s-2000s)

Tall and strong, he began his career in WCW as Alex Wright's bodyguard. He broke off on his own and was a steady independent star ever since. He died in 2004. [The Wall; Sgt. A-Wall; Snuff]

Mantel, Dutch
(1970s-2000s)

Named after an early century grappler of the same name, Dirty Dutch was a pure hell-raiser. Southern-based, the hairy-backed, bullwhip-wielding hellion had classic feuds with Jerry Lawler and Bill Dundee in the Mid-South region. He's been everywhere—from the NWA and WCW to SMW and WWF—and has been entertaining in all. [Uncle Zebekiah]

Markoff, Chris
(1960s-1980s)

The thick-bodied Markoff had solid runs in the AWA, WWA, and other Midwest groups throughout the 1960s. Yugoslavian-born, he entered the AWA as a singles star managed by Prof. Steve Druk and gained main-event status. His feuds against the Crusher drew large crowds. Later he teamed with Angelo Poffo in Indianapolis and finished his career as a Russian sympathizer.

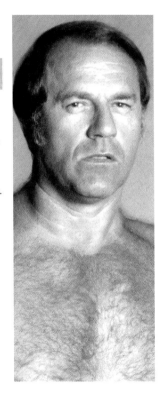

Marshall, Everett
(1920s-1930s)

With dashing looks, this youngster won the NWA championship in 1936, beating Ali Baba. He lost it to Lou Thesz in 1937 and the following year, with Steve Casey unable to defend the title, Marshall was given the belt by the NWA. In 1939, he lost it again to Thesz. Sadly, the talented wrestler was robbed of his fame early on due to injuries suffered in a car accident.

Martel, Rick
(1970s-1990s)

Martel, widely known for his WWF gimmick as the Model was actually a gifted technical star in the 1980s and a former AWA world champion. Trained by the Rougeaus, he won numerous Canadian belts before hitting the AWA in the early 1980s. In 1984, he beat Jumbo Tsuruta for that group's title. Few threw dropkicks with the proficiency of Martel. He ventured to the WWF where he teamed with Tom Zenk and Tito Santana, winning the world tag titles in 1987, before resuming a singles career. [The Model]

Rick Martel (left) and Roddy Piper get ready for action.

A poolside Rick Martel catches a few rays.

Martel, Sherri
(1980s-1990s)

One female wrestler who, by all accounts, was better than most men in the ring was Martel, a former AWA women's champion who trained under the Fabulous Moolah. Wonderfully talented, she shelved her wrestling career to become a valet in the AWA and WWF, guiding Buddy Rose, Doug Somers, and later, Shawn Michaels.

Martin, Judy
(1960s-1980s)

After plying her trade in the AWA and Mid-Atlantic areas, she caught on with the MTV/Cyndi Lauper craze in the 1980s. This long-time ally of Fabulous Moolah had numerous title shots against Wendi Richter for the WWF title.

Martinez, Pedro
(1960s-1970s)

This former promoter of the IWA (based in Cleveland) was a popular attraction in that region during the 1960s. His son, Pedro Martinez Jr., also wrestled.

Mascaras, Mil
(1960s-2000s)

Aaron Rodriguez was a bodybuilder chosen by an entertainment firm to play Mil in Mexican movies. Based on that success, he became an international draw in the 1970s. In the U.S., he was used as a special attraction. In the mid-1970s, he had his biggest chance at American stardom as the champion of the IWA. His name, loosely translated as "Man of a thousand masks," underscored his legend: He's reportedly never worn the same mask twice.

Masked Assassins, The
(1960s-1980s)

Although nearly every territory has at one time in the past used some
sort of Assassins gimmick, the most famous twosome was Jody Hamilton
and Tom Renesto Sr. The two were capable in the ring and performed
in Mid-Atlantic, Mid-South, and Florida. Don Bass was also a short-term
member of the team.

Maynard, Earl
(1960s-1970s)

An all-American looking good guy, the muscular Mr. America contestant headlined in Los Angeles in the 1970s. With Rocky Johnson, he won the Americas tag-team title. He was also a "Beat the Champ" titleholder in 1971.

Mazurki, Mike
(1930s-1950s)

Called "Iron Mike" in his wrestling days, he used his character-filled face and Hollywood connections to get himself (and fellow wrestlers of the 1950s and 1960s) coveted roles in television shows, "Charlie's Angels," and "Bonanza," and in films like Blood Alley, and Murder My Sweet." The Austrian-born Mazurki also co-founded the honorable Cauliflower Alley Club for retired wrestlers.

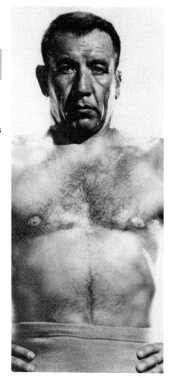

McDaniel, Ed "Wahoo"
(1960s-1990s)

Regarded as the finest Native American star to ever wrestle, McDaniel was a pro football star for the New York Jets and Miami Dolphins and trained for wrestling part time in the off-season with the Funks in Texas. Determined to bring respect and honor to his heritage, he was a proud fighter across the Mid-Atlantic, NWA, and AWA regions. He passed away in 2002 at the age of 63.

McIntyre, Velvet
(1970s-1980s)

This tireless world traveler caught on as part of the WWF's mid-1980s angles on MTV. She was a championship contender in the AWA and WWF. Among her opponents were Wendi Richter and Judy Martin.

McMahon, Stephanie
(1990s-2000s)

Her early days were spent as a fumbling girl, but Stephanie has grown into a respectable on-screen personality. She's been linked romantically with Triple H, and in addition to her roles on television, she is in charge of WWE's advertising unit.

McMahon Jr., Vince
(1970s-2000s)

Is he the greatest wrestling promoter of all-time? History will likely remember him that way. Vince took over the reigns of his father's company in the early 1980s and molded it into a Fortune 500 company. McMahon was once listed as a legit billionaire. His family has a rich tradition in wrestling. Despite his age, McMahon is a well-conditioned fitness fanatic and he held his company's world title in 1999 and has had ring feuds with Steve Austin, Triple H, Hulk Hogan, and his son, Shane McMahon.

McMahon Sr., Vince
(1960s-1980s)

Vince Sr. adopted Vince Jr. and sold his company to his son in the early 1980s. Before the current WWE product, Vince Sr. supplied the Washington and New York markets with consistent regional acts like Killer Kowalski and Bruno Sammartino to tremendous success. The New York icon passed away in 1984 from cancer.

Menaker, Sam
(1940s-1980s)

Slammin' Sam did it all. In addition to wrestling, he was a pro ballplayer in the Yankees organization, but after World War II, he turned his attention to wrestling promoting and managing. He helped promote Dick the Bruiser's WWA from 1964-87. In Chicago, he was a wrestling play-by-play announcer with baseball legend Joe Garagiola and Hall of Fame announcer Jack Brickhouse. Menacker also made his way to Hollywood, where he had parts in "Alias the Champ" and "Mighty Joe Young."

Mercer, Bill
(1970s-1980s)

A legendary wrestling announcer for the Von Erich's World Class group in Dallas, Mercer was a renowned sports announcer in Texas. To his credit, he has announced on radio for Texas pro teams, the Cowboys and Rangers (as a partner with Don Drysdale). He also called two Super Bowls and was inducted into the Texas Radio Hall of Fame.

Mero, Marc
(1990s-2000s)

Formerly an amateur boxer, he was discovered in the early 1990s and trained to wrestle in WCW as a novelty act. Funny though, his Johnny B. Badd character worked. Rather than stay in WCW, he took the money and ran for the WWF. But with a new gimmick, he failed to live up to the hype, although in 1996 he won the Intercontinental title. Perhaps he's best known for doing something away from wrestling: He married Sable. [Johnny B. Badd]

Mero, Rena
(1990s)

From trailer park to millionaire diva, the ex-wife of Marc Mero never wanted to get into wrestling, but couldn't resist the offer the WWF made her. With her runway model looks, she became a major player and Playboy pinup. In her few wrestling appearances, she actually fared well for someone without formal training. But it all crumbled for her when she departed the company claiming sexual harassment. However, in 2003, she made her return and apparently all was forgotten. [Sable]

Michaels, Shawn
(1980s-2000s)

The Heartbreak Kid has been a tremendous showman in the WWF. The San Antonio native, trained by Jose Lothario, broke in as a lightweight in the Central States area. Going nowhere fast, he teamed with Marty Jannetty and went to the AWA. They won the 1987 tag title. After hitting the WWF with Jannetty he was determined to be a singles star. He set out to prove himself in every match, having four-star bouts with Bret Hart, Mr. Perfect, and Razor Ramon. He was a three-time Intercontinental champ and three-time world champion. After early retirement, he came back and won the 2002 world title.

Midnight Express, The
(1980s-1990s)

In the early 1980s, up-and-coming manager Jim Cornette needed a team to send him to success. In Memphis, all the parts were around him. Dennis Condrey, Randy Rose, and Norvell Austin, teaming as the Midnight Express, had feuded with teams led by Stan Lane and Bobby Eaton. Cornette had a eureka moment. He put Condrey and Eaton together as the Express. Although Cornette's version of the Express also included Lane, his tandems won tag-team titles in Mid-South, World Class, and the NWA, where they were two-time world champs. They were often viewed as the greatest tag team ever.

Miller, Bill
(1950s-1960s)

Miller had a strong career using his own name. But to enhance his marketability, he invaded the AWA under a mask as Mr. M. In 1962, he beat Verne Gagne for the world title, but he was stripped of the belt eight months later when his true identity was revealed. [Mr. M]

Missing Link, The
(1970s-1980s)

Dewey Robertson broke into wrestling comparatively late in life and performed well into his 40s. His career took on new meaning as the Missing Link, a strange gimmick that saw him paint his face green and blue. He energized crowds in Mid-South, World Class, and WWF. [Dewey Robertson]

Monsoon, Gorilla
(1960s-1990s)

Before he died in 1999, Gorilla was the television face of the WWF. He was a wrestler, booker, road agent, announcer, and even co-owner of the WWF. As a wrestler in the 1960s and 1970s, Monsoon was billed as being from Mongolia, but his roots were in New Jersey. He had runs as champion in Los Angeles, Japan, and Australia, and later in his career, he and Bobby Heenan were a popular broadcast duo.

Moondogs, The
(1970s-2000s)

Is the Moondog one of the most emulated gimmicks ever? Carrying bones, wearing mangy outfits, and barking at the moon, no fewer than 10 Moondogs have hit the scene at one time or another. The most famous, the white-haired, bearded Lonnie Mayne, was a star in the Northwest and California. The Memphis area has been home to its share of Moondogs. Larry Latham and Wayne Ferris wrestled there and were noted for out-of-the-ring brawls. Southeast star Randy Colley was another. Well into the 1990s, the gimmick was still used and it's likely to stay for years to come.

Mr. Fuji
(1960s-1990s)

Contemporary fans remember this cane-wielding Japanese manager from the WWF, but Fuji was once an accomplished wrestler. Along his career, he was a five-time WWF tag-team champion—three times with Toru Tanaka and twice with Mr. Saito. His broken English was a hoot in interviews.

Mr. T.
(1980s-1990s)

Larry Tero made the most of every break he got. The former "A-Team" star was discovered during a tough-man contest and recruited to Hollywood. He crossed over to wrestling in 1984 as Hulk Hogan's training buddy for Wrestlemania. Since then, Mr. T has made numerous cameos in WWF and WCW as a wrestler and referee.

Mr. Wrestling
(1960s-1980s)

This masked star, named Tim Woods, followed in the masked Destroyer's footsteps. He was a staple in Georgia and Florida. His plain white mask, trunks, and boots were his trademarks. He also had a memorable feud with Ric Flair.

Mr. Wrestling II
(1970s-1980s)

Johnny Walker replaced Woods in the Georgia territory using his gimmick—despite being more than 40 years old at the time—and became even more popular than his predecessor. It is said one of his matches on cable was the first to draw more than a million viewers. [Rubberman; The Grappler]

Muchnick, Sam
(1930s-1980s)

A legendary promoter from St. Louis, his shows had strong NWA ties but he used a wide array of talent. For years, St. Louis wrestling was regarded as the best found anywhere and Muchnick made sure of that. Legends like Pat O'Connor, Dan Hodge, Lou Thesz, and Harley Race usually saved their best performances for Muchnick. His television shows, "Wrestling from the Chase Hotel," are still considered classics. He died in 1998.

Mulligan, Blackjack
(1970s-1980s)

Mulligan was a former football player with the New York Jets and set out for a career in wrestling. Eventually, he took on this Texan gimmick and cruised to a successful career. At 6-8 and 250 pounds, he and Blackjack Lanza were WWWF tag-team champions and he's the father of Barry and Kendall Windham. [Big Machine; Big Bob Windham]

Muraco, Don
(1980s-1990s)

He began as a Tom Selleck wannabe from Hawaii, but he turned rule breaker and bulked up considerably. He was an abrasive heel in Florida and Georgia and later a WWF Intercontinental champion before retiring with his wit intact.

Mutoh, Keiji
(1980s-2000s)

Mutoh is one of the few Japanese stars to break through in the U.S. After he turned pro, he ventured to North America. Wearing face paint, Ninja pants and spewing green mist, he was a hit as the Great Muta. With stints in Puerto Rico and World Class, he was ready for WCW in 1989. He wowed crowds with his moonsaults and beat Sting for the TV title. Frustrated, he headed back to Japan as a star and won the prestigious IWGP title on two occasions. [Great Muta; Super Black Ninja; White Ninja]

Mysterio Jr., Rey
(1990s-2000s)

A second-generation star from San Diego by way of Tijuana, he has been a spectacular junior heavyweight with cat-like responses. He was active in Mexico and Japan before getting a break in 1996 in WCW, where he held the cruiserweight title. His uncle is Rey Mysterio Sr.

Nash, Kevin
(1990s-2000s)

Discovered in a Georgia cannery and summoned to try wrestling, the nearly 7-foot-tall Nash had already played college hoops at Tennessee. Once in wrestling, he masterminded his way to the world title in WWF and WCW. But first he worked his way up the ladder as a prelim bum and bodyguard before breaking out on his own. In 1996, he was lured to WCW with Scott Hall where he formed the mega-successful NWO. [Master Blaster; Oz; Vinnie Vegas; Big Daddy Cool; Diesel]

Nasty Boys, The
(1980s-1990s)

Brian Knobbs and Jerry Saggs made up this strange duo. Originally, they were unorthodox and clumsy, but under the tutelage of Brad Rheingans, they improved and won world tag-team titles in the WWF and WCW and numerous regional groups. Wearing black T-shirts spray painted with their names, they were a grubby-looking team with a penchant for throwing chairs and using foreign objects. Knobbs went on to a singles career after Saggs retired due to an injury.

*At top: Brian Knobbs;
bottom: Jerry Saggs*

New World Order
(1990s)

Arguably, one of the most lucrative creations in wrestling history, the original trio of Scott Hall, Kevin Nash, and Hulk Hogan set WCW ablaze and gave the promotion life, with more than a year's worth of feuds and angles. They invaded "Monday Nitro" in 1996 and the company took off. When the NWO faded, so did WCW's run.

Niedhart, Jim
(1980s-2000s)

Nicknamed the "Anvil,"
he trained under the Hart
family in Calgary. Known
for his trademark goatee,
he traveled to regional
territories like Calgary and
Mid-South in the early
1980s, but was a hit in the
WWF as Bret Hart's partner
in the Hart Foundation,
winning the tag-team
championship twice.

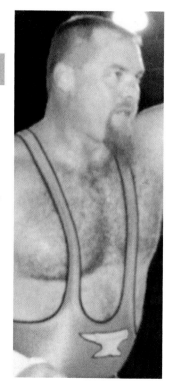

Norton, Scott
(1980s-2000s)

Former bouncer and arm wrestler turned ring wrestler, his success can't be denied. This bulky bruiser saw good times in Japan winning the IWGP title two times (1998 and 2001). He trained with the Gagne family's AWA and had success there in addition to WCW.

O'Connor, Pat
(1950s-1960s)

This famed NWA champion hailed from New Zealand. He won the belt in 1959 from Dick Hutton. He was a shooter-type wrestler who always played the good guy and his matches were commonly 45- to 60-minute performances. He had epic battles with Lou Thesz and Gene Kiniski in St. Louis.

O'Haire, Sean
(1990s-2000s)

WCW Power Plant grad who was a former tag-team champ of that group. He's very tall and has a super look that makes people believe he has a tremendous future in his current home, WWE.

Okerlund, Gene
(1970s-2000s)

The mustached "Mean Gene" was an ad executive who shared office space with the AWA when he was discovered to be a super pitchman on television. From the AWA, he leaped to the WWF and became famous for his interviewing chemistry on-screen with personalities like Hulk Hogan and Bobby Heenan.

Orndorff, Paul
(1970s-1990s)

Legit tough guy with a football background with the Atlanta Falcons, the rugged Orndorff plied his trade throughout the country with stops in Florida and Georgia before heading to WWF in the early 1980s. There, he feuded with Hulk Hogan to numerous sell-out crowds. A former two-time WCW tag champ with Paul Roma, he remained active well into the late 1990s, despite an injury which severely limited his arm strength.

Orton Jr., Bob
(1970s-1990s)

An underrated second-generation technician, Orton was a steady tag-team partner and talented enough to be a single's threat, although major singles titles always eluded him. A former NWA tag champ with Don Kernodle, he was a valuable part of the WWF's explosion in the 1980s, as he teamed with Roddy Piper and Adrian Adonis. His father is Bob Orton Sr.

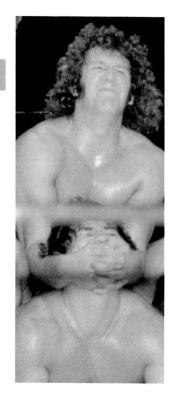

Orton Sr., Bob
(1950s-1970s)

The Texas-bred cowboy main evented throughout the world. He's the head of a three-generation household; his sons, Bob Jr. and Barry, and grandson, Randy, have all wrestled. Bob Sr. found most of his success in Texas, California, Canada, and the Gulf States, also as the masked Zodiac. In Kansas, he won the NWA Heart of America title in the early 1950s. [The Zodiac]

Page, Diamond Dallas
(1980s-2000s)

A miraculous person who started as a manager but rode his desire all the way to the world title, Page ran a nightclub in Florida when he was bit by the wrestling bug. He eventually managed stars like Badd Company in the AWA and Scott Hall in WCW. In the mid-1990s, he began wrestling and worked his way up the ladder. In 1999, he beat Ric Flair for his first of three WCW world titles. He retired in 2002.

Palumbo, Chuck
(1990s-2000s)

This tall, sculptured, newcomer had quick success, winning the tag titles in WCW with Sean O'Haire. He ventured to WWE where he has been a bit player, teaming with Billy Gunn, and Nunzio in a "Sopranos" gimmick.

Parisi, Tony
(1960s-1970s)

Popular Pennsylvania Italian who was the quintessential tag-team partner, he made a name for himself in the WWWF. In 1975, Parisi and Louis Cerdan shocked the world by winning the world tag belts over the powerful Blackjacks, Mulligan and Lanza. [Tony Pugliese]

Parks, Reggie
(1960s)

In tests of strength, the straight-ahead strongman was known for allowing cars to drive over his iron-like stomach. He was a top AWA draw and remains active today as a championship belt maker.

Patera, Ken
(1970s-1990s)

A former competitive weightlifter, Patera was discovered in televised strongman contests. He broke into wrestling in the AWA and traveled around the country. He often headlined Madison Square Garden and was the WWF Intercontinental champion in 1980, a title he held for eight months.

Patterson, Pat
(1960s-2000s)

Patterson, a top singles draw from Canada, had success in San Francisco in the 1960s. Widely known for his ring ability, he was a longtime tag partner with Ray Stevens. He once held the WWWF North American title in 1979, before it was renamed the Intercontinental championship. Famous for his classic Boot Camp match with Sgt. Slaughter, he stayed with the WWE and has been a booker and road agent since his retirement from the ring in the early 1980s.

Patterson, Peggy
(1970s-1980s)

This women's blonde bomber was billed as Pat Patterson's sister and was often the holder of versions of the women's title. She was well-schooled and had some matches with Madusa Micelli early in Madusa's career.

Pedicino, Joe
(1980s-1990s)

Pedicino was an adequate announcer who first became known for his syndicated show, "This Week in Pro Wrestling." He and co-host (and wife) Bonnie Blackstone built on that success and worked for WCW. Adept at television production, Pedicino took over the USWA in Texas, renamed it the Global Wrestling Federation, and tried his hand promoting on the ESPN Network. In later years, he was still working on a wrestling radio show from his native Georgia.

Pesek, John
(1920s-1940s)

Known as the Tigerman, he was considered a "ripper." A ripper was known to demolish his opponents in quick order. Though he never held a world title, he is widely remembered as a fabulous pure wrestler in his day. In addition to wrestling, he had an interest in greyhound racing. His son, Jack, wrestled and promoted in Nebraska.

Pillman, Brian
(1980s-1990s)

After a pro football stint, Pillman trained in Calgary, where he was taken in by the Hart family. He was a potent flyer and teamed with Bruce Hart as Bad Company in Stampede. He was signed to WCW in 1988, where he won the WCW tag titles (with Steve Austin) and also was the group's first cruiserweight champ. After a devastating car accident, Pillman's career faded. He was one of the most well-liked wrestlers when he passed away in 1998. [Yellow Dog; Flyin' Brian]

Piper, Roddy
(1970s-2000s)

The "Rowdy Scot" turned
pro at age 16 after spending
time homeless as a teen.
That proved to be his calling,
as Piper, born Roderick
Toombs, is one of wrestling's
most bombastic personalities
ever. From his beginnings
in Oregon and California,
he was the No. 1 heel in
Georgia and the WWF for
almost a decade. He's a two-
time Northwest and three-
time U.S. champion. Some
say, without Piper, the WWE
would not have been what
it is today.

Poffo, Angelo
(1960s-1980s)

The father of Randy Savage and Lanny Poffo, this patriarch was one of the most well-conditioned athletes of any era. He even claims numerous world records for push-ups and sit-ups. His ring career peaked in the 1970s, but despite his age, he wrestled until the 1980s. In addition to his ring duties, he founded the ICW in the 1970s and battled over promotional turf with rival Memphis promoters Nick Gulas and Jerry Jarrett. Jarrett ended up buying the group, leading to an ICW-CWA angle.

Poffo, Lanny
(1980s-1990s)

This second-generation performer didn't have success like his father or brother, Randy Savage, but he had a lengthy career. Lanny was the polar opposite of his mouthy, flamboyant sibling. With Savage, he held the Southern tag-team title in Memphis and had memorable bouts with the Nightmares and Rock & Roll Express. Poffo bolted for the WWF in 1985 and was used as an opening act. He also had a penchant for reciting poems when he later managed Curt Hennig. [The Genius]

Precious
(1980s)

This dainty 1980s valet (and wife) of Jimmy Garvin sprayed the ring with disinfectant prior to Garvin's arrival. She was the source of much mayhem while in Dallas and the NWA.

Pritchard, Tom
(1980s-2000s)

With a wit like Roddy Piper, he was a classic Southern pest and was a consummate tag-team wrestler. After wrestling well over a decade, including time in the WWF, he has become a WWE talent coordinator. [Zip; Dr. of Desire] See: Heavenly Bodies; Body Donnas.

Race, Harley
(1950s-1990s)

The Kansas City native was a classy, eight-time NWA world champion. Before Ric Flair, the NWA was identified by Race's skills. His wrestling career began in the 1950s and along the way he held titles in nearly every region of the country. A three-time Missouri champion, he wrestled Ric Flair at the first Starrcade in 1983. He moved on to the WWF, where he wrestled as the King, but he never duplicated his NWA success. [King Harley Race]

Raven
(1980s-2000s)

Originally a bratty heel, Raven has gone through many changes in his career. In Portland, he was a mile-a-minute talker. He won that title three times. He had a brief early stint in WWF, but didn't hit his stride until hooking up with ECW in the early 1990s. He transformed himself into the loner, Raven, and the feuds with Tommy Dreamer and Sandman still have fans talking. [Scott Levy; Scotty the Body; Johnny Polo]

Ray, Stevie
(1990s)

Originally from the Texas independents, Ray was the powerful partner to his real-life brother, Booker T, in their team, Harlem Heat. He developed most of his skills on live TV. When Booker took off for greener pastures, Ray was left out. Before WCW closed, he tried his hand at television commentary.

Red Cloud, Billy
(1950s-1960s)

A cruiserweight before his time, this Native American mastered the chop. The Mohawk-sporting wrestler was a popular prelim and tag-team performer.

Reed on left, Ron Simmons on right.

Reed, Butch
(1970s-1990s)

This former rodeo circuit performer and football player turned to pro wrestling in the late 1970s. A super heel in Central States, Calgary, Florida and Georgia with dyed hair, he turned to the WWF in the mid-1980s and then to WCW, where he teamed with Ron Simmons to win the world tag titles. [Bruce Reed; Hacksaw Reed; The Natural]

Regal, William
(1980s-2000s)

This well-schooled European wrestler began on the carnival circuit in England. He was lured to America by WCW and had quick success there in 1993, winning the TV title. He eventually won the belt three times. Known for his witty facial expressions, he fit right in with the WWE. There, he won the European title twice and admirably fought back from a public fight with substance abuse. [Lord Steven Regal]

Renegade, The
(1990s)

Independent wrestler Richard Wilson got the break he always wanted as a knock-off of the Ultimate Warrior. Promoters believed in him and in 1995, he beat Arn Anderson for the WCW TV title. With his flash-in-the-pan career seemingly over, his inner demons sadly led him to commit suicide in 1999.

Rhodes, Dustin
(1980s-2000s)

Few wrestlers today have a connection to the outlaw days of Terry Funk and Dick Murdoch, but count Dustin, the son of Dusty Rhodes, as one of them. His Texas roots have served him well. Although he was never a mega-star, his consistency has been a benefit. Dustin moved to WCW at a young age, but hung in there, winning the U.S. and world tag titles. Even outlaws are susceptible to changes, and since the late 1990s, he's played the face-painted Goldust character in WWE.

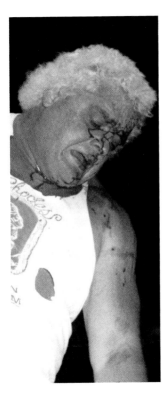

Rhodes, Dusty
(1960s-2000s)

Fans of his early work know him as one of the most dramatic and fiery interviews ever. Named for a 1950s baseball hero, Dusty played football and baseball in college and pined to be a pro wrestler. Big money feuds have followed him to every territory. In Florida, from 1973-82, he held the Florida Southern title nine times. In NWA country, Rhodes earned icon status, and in 1979, he won his first of three world titles. In the mid-1980s, he added matchmaking to his resume. He's credited with creating the War Games cage matches and the Great American Bash summer series. [Midnight Rider; American Dream]

An embattled Rusty Rhodes inside the ring.

Rich, Tommy
(1970s-2000s)

"Wildfire," has been one of the more passionate performers of the last 25 years. In 1981, he shocked the world by becoming the youngest man ever to hold the NWA world title when he dethroned Harley Race. Although he held the belt for only a week, the win cemented his legend. Known for a wide array of scientific moves, he also held the Georgia National title. Since the 1980s, Rich has had an on-and-off career in the Mid-South and Memphis areas. Tommy's brother, Johnny, also wrestled.

Richter, Wendi
(1980s-1990s)

The former Dallas Cowgirl was an overnight sensation in the mid-1980s thanks to MTV and Cindy Lauper. Fiery and fun loving, Richter dethroned the Fabulous Moolah from her 30-year reign as world women's champion as part of the "Rock & Wrestling" explosion of the early 1980s.

Rikidozan
(1950s)

Long considered the father of pro wrestling in Japan, the Korean-born wrestler named Sin-Nak Kim had "pro" exhibitions for a nation accustomed to sumo. Thousands would see the exhibitions and "poof!" a new sport was born. He brought in larger-than-life foes like Lou Thesz, the Destroyer, Fred Blassie, and the Sheik, and his fan base grew incredibly. His understudies, Giant Baba and Antonio Inoki, went on to prominence after Rikidozan's murder in 1963 at age 39.

Rikishi
(1980s-2000s)

One of many Samoan wrestlers in the WWE, he was originally a member of the Samoan Swat Team and Headshrinkers in World Class, WCW, and the WWF. For a 400-pound man, he has the quickness of a cruiserweight. As a singles star, he always struggled, before landing headlong into the Rikishi character. After some initial trepidation, he committed to the part and never looked back. [Fatu; The Sultan]

Road Warriors, The
(1980s-2000s)

When then-Georgia promoter Ole Anderson wanted a new gimmick for the 1980s, little did he know his request would result in the Warriors. Hawk and Animal, with characters based around the movie "Road Warrior," revolutionized wrestling with their persona and power. The entire decade belonged to them, as virtually every arena they appeared in drew thousands to see their unique style. Managed by Paul Ellering, they were the first team to capture all Big Three (AWA, NWA, and WWF) tag titles. [Legion of Doom; LOD]

Roberts, Buddy
(1970s-1990s)

Dazed and confused as a singles star, he found a niche as a tag-team worker. Roberts teamed first with Jerry Brown as the Hollywood Blondes; he then joined Terry Gordy and Michael Hayes as the Fabulous Freebirds. He was a bit small and not overly charismatic, but as part of a team, he was a fine complement. [Dale Valentine]

Roberts, Jake
(1980s-2000s)

The son of Grizzly Smith, Roberts has lived a very public life filled with drug addiction, as chronicled in the film, "Beyond the Mat." In his heyday, Roberts was known as the great ring psychologist and storyteller. Few wrestlers cut more believable promos than Roberts. He wrestled all over the country before reaching superstar status in the WWF during the 1980s. Although he never carried a major belt there, he was often as popular as Randy Savage and Hulk Hogan—perhaps even more so.

Robinson, Billy
(1950s-1980s)

The English shooter was a regional titleholder in Britain, Japan, Canada and Texas before settling in the AWA. There, he held the tag titles with Verne Gagne and the Crusher. He even had some 60-minute matches with Gagne. In Japan, he feuded with Rikidozan. He's remembered as one of the toughest wrestlers to go up against.

Rocco, Mark
(1970s-1990s)

A tremendously skilled British star, his technical ability was praised worldwide in the 1980s. Although he didn't have a career in the U.S., Rocco was a terrific heel in the U.K. and his reputation was cemented in a series of matches in Japan as the Black Tiger against the original Tiger Mask (Satoru Sayama). In England, he feuded with Sammy Lee (Sayama) and Keiji Yamada (Jushin Liger). In the early 1980s, he was a three-time world heavy middleweight champion and often teamed with Fit Finlay. [Rollerball Rocco; Black Tiger]

Rock & Roll Express, The
(1980s-2000s)

Two prelim light heavyweights, Ricky Morton and Robert Gibson, were lost as singles stars when Jerry Lawler combined them as this rocking tag team. In 1984, everyone wanted a piece of them. They were the precursors to today's faster-paced teams like the Hardy Boys. Gibson was a solid worker, but the team revolved around Morton, who had tremendous skill and popularity. The duo could wrestle anyone, from the Russians to the Four Horsemen to the Midnight Express. They rode that success to Memphis, Mid-South, Mid-Atlantic, and the NWA, where they were four-time NWA tag-team champions.

Rock, The
(1990s-2000s)

Dwayne Johnson is one of the most talked about wrestlers of all time. He's a third-generation star, as his father Rocky Johnson and granddad Peter Maivia were ring stars from the 1950s to 1980s. He's done everything, from winning the world title to starring in a motion picture, and sitting next to President George W. Bush. But it all started innocently enough. A football player at the University of Miami, he abandoned his sports career to be become a wrestler. His early trainers saw his potential, and he was sent to Memphis to learn the ropes. He was then sent to the WWF, where he became who he is today. [Flex Cavana]

Rockers, The
(1980s-1990s)

A high-energy tag team that turned the undersized Marty Jannetty and Shawn Michaels into international superstars. Alone, both wrestlers were floundering in the early 1980s when they were matched together in the AWA as the Midnight Rockers. There, they won the AWA tag-team titles and feuded with Buddy Rose and Doug Somers. The lure of the WWF was too great and by the late 1980s, they departed the AWA. In the WWF, and renamed The Rockers, the duo had classic matches with The Brainbusters and The Hart Foundation. See: Marty Jannetty; Shawn Michaels.

Rogers, Buddy
(1950s-1970s)

Rogers, the first "Nature Boy," was also the first-ever WWWF champion in 1963, as well as a former NWA world champion (1961-63). He was proficient at roughhousing and submission holds, but was also known for his sense of timing. He was one of the great blond-haired heels of his day. His look took him to Hollywood, where he found work on several TV shows. After his WWWF title loss to Bruno Sammartino in 1963, Rogers was forced to retire because of heart trouble. He died in 1992 at age 71.

Rogers, Rip
(1970s-1990s)

A highly conditioned prelim star who had regional fame in the 1980s, his blond hair and pink outfits were always a sight to see. He had runs in Continental and Memphis and always remained old school. Since his wrestling days, he's been a trainer at the Ohio Valley Wrestling facility near his home state, Indiana.

Roma, Paul
(1980s-1990s)

Roma had better-than-average talent and a movie-star look. In the 1980s, he was a young up-and-comer who teamed with Jim Powers as the jobber team, the Young Stallions. He finally had a chance to hold a major tag title in the early 1990s as the tag-team partner of Paul Orndorff in WCW. Very athletic, he tried his hand at boxing and retired with a 2-1 pro record.

Rose, Buddy
(1970s-1990s)

A noted mid-card performer, the rotund Rose was a talented worker and eight-time Portland champion where he also feuded with Roddy Piper and Jay Youngblood. Always good for a laugh on interviews, he is a former AWA tag-team champion with Doug Somers.

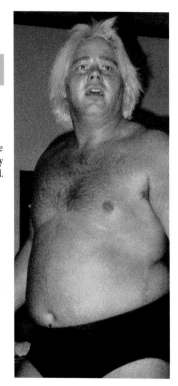

Ross, Jim
(1970s-2000s)

Even Ross would likely tell you his success couldn't have been predicted. The former college football announcer first joined Bill Watts' Mid-South group to supplement his income. The wrestling business would be his home for the next 20 years, where his influence can't be undervalued. Held in the highest regard, along with Gordon Solie and Jack Brickhouse, he's been the standard-setter for new announcers. He's called hundreds of NWA and WWE world title matches and has been the lead host for the WWE since 1997. Even a severe case of Bells Palsy, which forced to him to relearn his verbal skills, couldn't hide his talents.

Rotten, Axl
(1980s-2000s)

A toned-down version of his brother, Ian, Axl is very hardcore, nonetheless. Based out of the Mid-South, the rotund punk rocker won the Global tag-team titles with Ian, and then feuded with him. He struggled to become a household name, but nearly became mainstream while in ECW as the partner of Balls Mahoney. But is there life after hardcore for Axl?

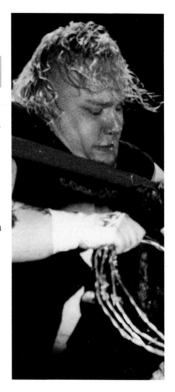

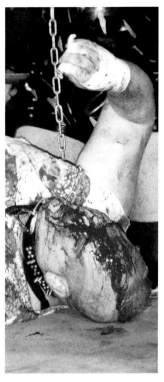

Rotten, Ian
(1980s-2000s)

Not as well-known nationally as his brother, Axl, this Rotten has led an infamous independent career. He runs a hardcore promotion in Kentucky-Indiana that takes garbage wrestling to new heights. Rotten is usually at the center of all the mayhem.

Rotunda, Mike
(1980s-2000s)

A former Syracuse star who had a long and productive ring career. Always seen as a capable, technical star without a lot of flair, he spent many years in Japan and was a star in Florida and later the NWA and WWF. In 1985, he and Barry Windham won the WWF tag belts twice; in 1989, he and Steve Williams won the NWA world tag-team title. By the early 1990s, his career seemed on the downside, when he was rejuvenated. His stock rose and he was given another chance in the WWF. With Ted DiBiase, he was a three-time world tag champion from 1992-93. [Michael Wallstreet; Irwin R. Shyster]

Rude, Rick
(1980s-1990s)

Tough amateur arm wrestler and boxer, who was discovered as he was working as a nightclub bouncer. Rude, who was tall and had the most ripped abs of any modern-day wrestler, took pride in improving in the ring. With early success in Mid-South, World Class, and the NWA (where he was a world tag-team champion with Manny Fernandez), Rude bolted for the WWF. Good move. He became a viable main-event star who carried the company's Intercontinental title in 1989. In 1993, he held the WCW International title, which at the time was the company's lead belt, on two occasions. In 1998, in the midst of a comeback, he died at age 40.

Russell, Lance
(1960s-2000s)

Ask any longtime fan in the South their favorite memory, and this classy Memphis announcer will likely be part of it. Since the 1960s, the golden-throated Russell has been going strong as the voice of Memphis wrestling. He played a wonderful straight man to the heel Jerry Lawler in the King's formative years there. He's worked almost exclusively in Memphis; however, he did some work for WCW in the early 1990s.

Sabu
(1990s-2000s)

Terry Brunk, the pioneering table breaker from Detroit, is the nephew of the Sheik, Ed Farhat. Taking a wild page from his uncle, Sabu is nothing short of a wildman himself. He first found a home in Japan's FMW and ECW, where his suicidal tendencies were nurtured en-route to two-time ECW world singles and three tag-team titles. Although he never found major-league success—is he too wild?—he's never been one to bow to risks and is still active despite many injuries suffered over the years.

Saito, Masa
(1970s-2000s)

A classic Japanese star who was as stiff as they come, Saito had success in Japan and the U.S. His real fame came as part of the New Japan group, where he was a major star in the late 1980s, alongside Antonio Inoki and Tatsumi Fujinami. He had tours of the WWF (where he was a two-time tag champion with Mr. Fuji) and AWA, where he teamed with Ken Patera and Jesse Ventura. Later, in 1990, he returned to the group and won the world title from Larry Zbyszko. [Mr. Saito]

Sakata, Harold
(1950s-1960s)

What a noteworthy career this Hawaiian-born wrestler had. He was a hated Japanese character in wrestling and parlayed his image into a spot in the 1964 James Bond flick, "Goldfinger," as the top-hat wearing Oddjob. Many Asian stars wisely copied his tuxedo image, but none had his success. [Tosh Togo]

Sammartino, Bruno
(1960s-1980s)

The man from Abuzzi, Italy, was one of the most popular champions in the world. Though he toured occasionally through the AWA, NWA, and Japan, Bruno spent almost his entire career with the WWWF. He sold out Madison Square Garden regularly, as well as arenas in Philadelphia, Boston, and Pittsburgh. He was the first world champion of the company and held the belt continuously from 1963-71. His second run stretched from 1973-77. Sammartino broke ties with the company he helped build because he disagreed with the new direction wrestling took in the early 1980s.

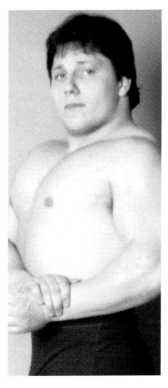

Sammartino, David
(1970s-1980s)

Like father, like son, sort of. David followed his pop's footsteps, but unfortunately never lived up to the name. He toured the country and even worked in the WWF with his father, Bruno. Because he was short and stocky, promoters didn't feel he had the goods to be a star. Eventually, he got burned out on wrestling and left the business entirely.

Sandman, The
(1990s-2000s)

With a gimmick for the times, Sandman was the king of hardcore on the East Coast during the 1990s. He cemented his legacy in ECW with his cigarette smoking, cane-winging gimmick. He won the company's world title five times from 1992-2001 and attained a cult following after his feuds with Raven and Tommy Dreamer. [Hardcore Hak]

Santana, Tito
(1970s-1990s)

One of the great baby faces, Merced Solis was a precursor to today's high flyers. In college, he played football at West Texas with Tully Blanchard and his athleticism was shown in his drop kicks. His wrestling stardom reached its pinnacle in the 1980s. After success in the AWA, he went to the WWF where he was both the Intercontinental and tag-team champion (with Rick Martel). Some say he never had a bad match. [El Matador; Merced Solis]

Tito Santana in action.

Savage, Randy
(1980s-2000s)

Family ties to wrestling and pure athleticism helped Savage grow into a superior talent in the late 20th Century. He was a minor league baseball player when his family ties came calling. As the son of legend Angelo Poffo and brother of Lanny Poffo, Savage was ready for prime time. His grinding voice and flamboyant Macho Man persona earned him a shot in the WWF in 1985. Promoters believed in him, as he earned both the WWF and WCW world titles. He's also headlined Wrestlemania. For much of his career, he was accompanied by his ex-wife, the late Miss Elizabeth.

Savannah Jack
(1980s)

A master of the superkick, Ted Russell joined Bill Watts' UWF after a tour with the Midwest independents. In the Mid-South, he was a brief popular attraction and battled Iceman Parsons and Buddy Roberts over the TV title. The former black belt in karate was also a Golden Gloves boxing champ. He retired early due to poor health.

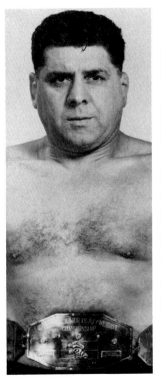

Savoldi, Angelo
(1950s-1990s)

This dad has been a constant on the Massachusetts scene, including in his own group, ICW, which was founded in 1985. The group closed a decade later, but his legacy is strong. As a wrestler, he was an NWA junior heavyweight champ. As a promoter, he had a unique pipeline to Puerto Rico and sometimes brought in Carlos Colon and Hercules Ayala to the Northeast. As a trainer, he's helped Ayala and his sons (Joe, Tom, and Mario) become wrestlers.

Savoldi, Joe
(1930s)

Controversy seemed to follow the original Joe Savoldi. He was an accomplished football player, having played at Notre Dame for Knute Rockne from 1928-30. He was expelled from the school for being married. In 1930, he played for the Bronko Nagurski-led Chicago Bears, but bolted the team after three games. With his famous dropkick, he turned to wrestling. In a famous 1932 bout with Jim Londos, Savoldi double-crossed Londos and laid claim to the world title. Savoldi eventually gave the belt back, but the controversy caused such uproar, wrestling was banned in Chicago for a brief time.

Sawyer, Buzz
(1970s-1980s)

This former amateur star lived fast and died young. At his best, he created a mad dog-like character. The suplex master, remembered as a short, fast-paced maniac who utilized the top rope well, his best years were in the early 1980s in Georgia, where he feuded with Tommy Rich over the Georgia National title.

Scorpio
(1990s-2000s)

A superb high flyer with Japanese training, Scorpio seemed destined for stardom. He had runs in WWF, WCW, and ECW and has had tremendous bouts with Chris Benoit, Dean Malenko, and Eddy Guerrero. A top competitor, he was once considered one of the best workers in the world. In 1993, he captured the WCW tag title with Marcus Bagwell. [2 Cold Scorpio; Flash Funk]

Sgt. Slaughter
(1980s-2000s)

Few wrestlers would have fit the bill as the "Sarge" as well as Bob Remus. Whether he was the half-crazed drill sergeant or the flag-waving fan favorite, he never lost a step. Remus began his career as the masked Super Destroyer. In the early 1980s, he established himself with the military gimmick while in the Mid-Atlantic area, often teaming with Don Kernodle. He toured often as both a heel and fan favorite, winning many titles along the way. None were bigger than the WWF crown, which he grabbed from the Ultimate Warrior in 1991 in a controversial Gulf War-inspired angle. [D.I. Bob Slaughter; Super Destroyer]

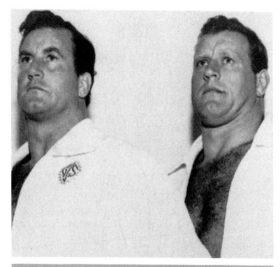

Sharpe Bros., The
(1950s-1960s)

The Ontario, Canada, tough guys, Ben and Mike, were big in the West. In San Francisco, they held the NWA tag titles 16 times. At nearly 7-feet-tall, they were a formidable team indeed. They also wrestled as the Harris Bros. Ben also had singles success as the NWA Hawaiian champ and Pacific Coast champion. They also wrestled together in Japan during the Rikidozan era.

Sharpe Jr., Mike
(1970s-1980s)

A borderline star with good size (6'5, 260 pounds) and lineage to boot. He was managed by Fred Blassie and the Grand Wizard during his WWF stints in the 1970s, but main-event status eluded him. After touring Canada, he returned to the WWF in the 1980s using a "loaded" wrist guard and nicknamed "Iron Mike."

Sheepherders, The
(1960s-1980s)

The Sheepherders were one of the most violent and bloody teams of any era. Lord Jonathan Boyd founded the group with Luke Williams. Their original matches bordered on R-rated exhibitions. When Boyd retired, Williams took on Butch Williams as his partner and the two picked up where Boyd left off. Feuds with the Fantastics, the Invaders, and the Samoans—actually anyone who dared to enter their world— are still considered classics.

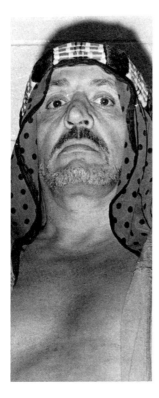

Sheik, The
(1950s-1990s)

Although he never held a major world recognized title in the AWA, WWF, or NWA, he was a top attraction in the 1960s and 1970s. Ed Farhat began his career as the Sheik and settled into a rulebreaking style. He used concealed weapons, fire, and chairs to dismantle his opponents. He mainly wrestled out of Detroit, but Farhat was a star in Los Angeles, Toronto and Tokyo. In Detroit, his feud with Bobo Brazil spilled into the aisles for nearly 10 years. Revered in Japan, he wrestled at age 65 with his nephew, Sabu, in a ring of fire match. After suffering severe burns, it proved to be the last match from the hardcore icon. But what other way would we expect the Sheik to end his career? In 2003, Farhat passed away. [Original Sheik]

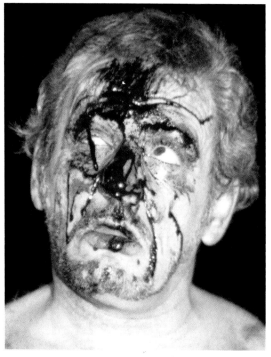

A blood-covered Sheik.

Simmons, Ron
(1980s-2000s)

Simmons, an All-American football star from Florida State, was the first African-American to hold the WCW/NWA world title, which he won 1992 from Vader. After football, he began his career in the Florida circuit, but he quickly moved to the NWA/WCW. Before his singles run, he held the world tag belts with Butch Reed as Doom. As his career wound down, he found a home in the WWE. [Farooq]

Singh, Makhan
(1980s-1990s)

Some consider Singh, along with Vader, as the best working big man in history. The 350-plus pounds wrestler was a hard worker in Canada in his feuds with the Harts. A multiple-time tag-team champion, he was the leader of a crew of Singhs in Calgary. The three-time Calgary champ had five-star matches against Owen Hart. In the early 1990s, he had popular runs in WCW as Norman the Lunatic and also spent time in the WWF. [Bastion Booger; Norman the Lunatic; Trucker Norm]

Singh, Tiger Jeet
(1960s-1980s)

Although Singh was a marginally talented ring worker, his bloody and maniacal style earned him main-event status the world over. The turban-wearing East Indian rulebreaker was linked to the Original Sheik as both partner and enemy. His epic wars harken to the days of Rikidozan. He was never a mainstream performer in the U.S., but he remains a mythical cult figure in Japan.

Skipper, Elix
(1990s-2000s)

A talented African American cruiserweight, Skipper has made a name for himself as a star with a lot of potential. His asset is his charisma, which draws comparisons to former football star Deion Sanders. He is a former WCW cruiserweight champion.

Slater, Dick
(1970s-1990s)

Tough as a Funk and ugly as George Steele, this Southern wrestler trained under Hiro Matsuda in Florida. In the 1980s, he was a widely used star in Florida and Mid-Atlantic. Not a headliner, he was a regular semi-main attraction. As tough as any wrestler to come from Texas, he often teamed with fellow Texans Dick Murdoch and Dusty Rhodes.

Smith, Davey Boy
(1980s-2000s)

Most know the Brit as a bulky WWF heavyweight, but Smith actually has roots as a junior heavyweight. In the beginning, he weighed around 160, but later bulked up to more than 250 pounds. His main fame came as one-half of the British Bulldogs with Dynamite Kid. The twosome were WWF tag-team champions in 1986. Smith had success as a singles star, after Kid retired, by winning the WWF Intercontinental title in 1992. He was also the first European champion in 1997. Before he died in 2002, he left the family legacy in the hands of his wrestling son, Harry Smith. [British Bulldog]

Smith, Johnny
(1980s-1990s)

This Calgary-based performer was billed as the cousin of Davey Boy Smith and was even considered a British Bulldog. Although he never caught on stateside, he successfully toured Singapore, England, Europe, Canada and Japan. His Japan bookings gave him a reputation as a hard worker. Those foreign influences served him well once back home, as he carried the British Commonwealth title three times in Stampede.

Smothers, Tracy
(1980s-2000s)

A friendly, Southern wrestler, Smothers made contributions in the Kentucky-West Virginia region. Closely aligned with the Armstrong family, he teamed with Steve Armstrong as the Southern Boys in WCW. As a singles star, Smothers held the Smoky Mountain title during the early 1990s. [Freddy Joe Floyd]

Snow, Al
(1980s-2000s)

This WWE employee can wrestle all styles. With gimmicks, he can be a psycho, goof ball, or father figure. A disciplined performer, he stuck to his guns until he was given a chance. After struggling in the independents, Snow found a home in Smoky Mountain and WWF with a variety of personas. He's a five-time hardcore champion and held the WWF tag title with Mick Foley in 1999. [Avatar; Leif Cassidy]

Snuka, Jimmy
(1970s-2000s)

The "Superfly" is easily one of the most recognizable stars of his era. The buffed, part Hawaiian was one of the first to use rope leaps to dazzle fans. He had success in Hawaii, Portland, and Japan, but his biggest success came in the WWF. Had Vince McMahon not had access to Hulk Hogan, Snuka was the promoter's second choice to take the WWF national in 1984. Even so, Snuka was closely aligned with the group's early national success. His feud with Roddy Piper still gets fans talking and his leaps.

Song, Pak
(1960s-1970s)

A native of Korea, he wrestled across the South and was an early partner of a then-heel Dusty Rhodes. On television, he would break wood and cement with his bare hands. After holding titles in Florida, he is remembered for putting Rhodes on the map. In a classic feud, Song turned on Rhodes, which gave Rhodes (renamed the American Dream) an amazing run as a fan favorite. Their feud drew sellouts in the Sunshine State for nearly half a year.

Sonnenberg, Gus
(1920s-1930s)

A Larry Zbyszko-looking wrestler, the former college football player helped solidify wrestling's image in the early days. He was immortalized after winning the NWA world title in 1929 from Strangler Lewis in Boston. He held the belt until losing it to Ed Don George in 1930.

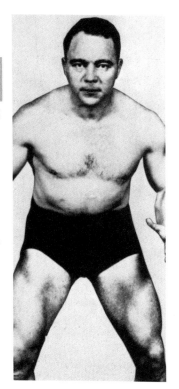

Stasiak, Shawn
(1990s-2000s)

Formerly an amateur wrestler, this second-generation son of Stan Stasiak cut his teeth in Memphis after training with the Funks. With Lex Luger looks, he visited WCW and WWF before fading into the sunset. [Meat; Perfectshawn]

Stasiak, Stan
(1960s-1970s)

The master of the heart punch, he shocked the world by defeating Pedro Morales for the WWWF world title in 1973. Although his reign was only nine days long—he dropped the belt to Bruno Sammartino—his name will forever be remembered. During the 1960s, he was a top Northwest attraction and had a rep as a tough tag-team wrestler. The old school roughneck is the father of Shawn Stasiak.

Steamboat, Ricky
(1970s-1990s)

The Verne Gagne-trained performer, born Richard Blood, was a fan favorite virtually his entire career. His training days were spent with another future star, Ric Flair. Ironically, the two would forever be known for their matches against each other. Capitalizing on the Steamboat name, Ricky was a compelling 1980s wrestler. He concentrated his time in the Southeast and Mid-Atlantic regions. In 1989, his series of matches with Flair over the NWA world title put him in Hall of Fame contention. In 1989, they traded the NWA world title in a series that also boasted 60-minute draws around the country.

Stecher, Joe
(1910s-1930s)

One of the NWA's first champion and toughest wrestlers, Stecher was a three-time world champion in the late 1910s to 1920s. When the legend Frank Gotch retired, Stecher beat the recognized champion, Charlie Cutler, and was christened world champ by promoters in 1915. In 1916, he went to a classic five-hour draw with Strangler Lewis in Omaha. Stecher later beat Earl Caddock in 1920 and some 10 years removed from his first belt, he dethroned Stanislaus Zbyszko. Sadly, he spent the last 30 years of his life institutionalized with mental illness and passed away in 1974.

Steele, George
(1970s-1990s)

The former high school wrestling coach led an amazing pro-wrestling career. The hairy-bodied lunatic would eat turnbuckles, shout gibberish, and dye his tongue green. A true oddity, he was later used as a fan favorite in the WWF to rousing success.

Steiner, Rick
(1980s-1990s)

A graduate of Brad
Rheingan's camp, Rick hit
the road early and found
success in Bill Watts' UWF.
There, he was a maniac
teaming with Sting and Eddie
Gilbert. With the sale of the
UWF to the NWA, Steiner
became a staple for the major
group. Eventually, he teamed
with Steve Williams, Mike
Rotunda, and his brother,
Scott, who he enjoyed his
greatest success with. In all,
Rick has been an eight-time
world tag champion with his
brother.

Steiner, Scott
(1980s-2000s)

The younger brother of Rick Steiner, he was a standout at the University of Michigan where, in 1986, he finished in sixth place at the NCAA national championships in the 190-pound division. Closely aligned with his brother during his career, Scott has been a world title contender for more than a decade. He won eight tag-team titles with Rick. Once tabbed as the heir apparent to Ric Flair, he won the WCW world title in 2000 from Booker T. When he was smaller, he helped bring numerous aerial moves to the U.S. including the huricanrana. [Big Poppa Pump]

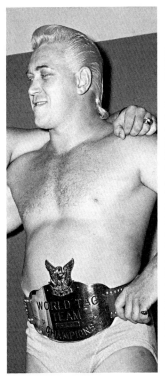

Stevens, Ray
(1960s-1980s)

After carving a niche as a rodeo rider and car racer, Stevens tried wrestling. His career began to evolve in the Memphis and Mid-South territories in the 1960s. Although he was a world traveler, he made a home in California where he met Pat Patterson and created a classic heel team. By the 1970s, the "Crippler's" career reached a new level. He was a four-time AWA tag-team champion with Nick Bockwinkel (3) and Patterson (1). Stevens is remembered as a legend in the industry. He died in 1996. [Ray Shire]

Sting
(1980s-2000s)

Steve Borden was discovered in California as part of Power Team USA, a weightlifting squad, and quickly broke off to Bill Watts' UWF with his original partner, the Ultimate Warrior, as the Blade Runners. When Warrior bolted, the face-painted Sting climbed the ladder in the NWA. An immediate fan favorite, he was given main-event status and positioned for a world title run. Despite a near-career ending knee injury, he recovered to beat Ric Flair in 1990 for his first of seven world titles.

*Sting prepares
to leave his
mark.*

Stomper, The
(1960s-1980s)

Archie Gouldie was one of the most well-conditioned athletes of any era. The former football player once set a world-record 2,800 sit-ups in one hour. Legend has it he once rode a bicycle from Arizona to Calgary, where he was an eight-time Stampede champion. He also toured around the South, including Tennessee, where he was a tag champion with Jos LeDuc, and in Georgia, where he was a National title holder. [Mongolian Stomper]

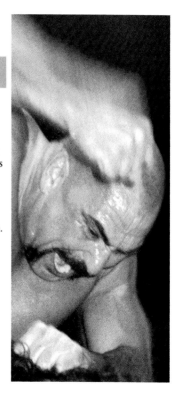

Storm, Lance
(1990s-2000s)

The proud Canadian, a fitness fanatic, broke into wrestling as Chris Jericho's friend and partner. He was at his best as a tag-team wrestler in ECW. Straight-laced, he's also held the WCW U.S. title. Fewer stars today can say they passed through the Hart family dungeon, but Storm can. In that sense, he's part of a dying breed.

Stratus, Trish
(1990s-2000s)

Former fitness model turned WWF valet and wrestler, Trish hails from Toronto. At the behest of Vince McMahon, she began training to be a wrestler. Determined to make it work, she worked her way to the WWE women's title and did so admirably.

Street, Adrian
(1970s-1980s)

Exotic Adrian was a genius whose gimmickry and ideas live today. Realizing his career was going nowhere, the Brit became the "Exotic One," a face-painted androgynous oddity. Part Alice Cooper, part Gorgeous George, he was an attraction in the Southeast including Florida and Alabama. The fine tactical wrestler even recorded several albums.

Stubbs, Jerry
(1970s-1980s)

Stubbs surely lived two lives in the ring. As the bald-headed Stubbs, he was a dreaded heel. But he had masked, heroic, alter egos named Mr. Olympia and The Matador. In all, he was a four-time Alabama heavyweight champion, four-time Southeast tag-team champion (three won with Arn Anderson), and a four-time Continental tag-team champ during a prolific career. [Matador; Mr. Olympia]

Pictured as Mr. Olympia.

Studd, John
(1970s-1980s)

One of the sport's legends, he was also considered a true gentleman despite being a heel in the ring. The protégé of Killer Kowalski, he won the WWWF tag title with Nikolai Volkoff as the masked Executioners in 1976. Studd, at 6-8, 350 pounds, was very impressive visually. He also feuded with Andre the Giant in the early 1980s. He died in 1995 at age 46 after a long illness. [Capt. USA; Executioner]

Sullivan, Kevin
(1970s-2000s)

The Bostonian has had a career full of twists and turns. He's been a wrestler more than four decades, but his biggest contributions have been backstage. He began as a muscular hero in Georgia, but soon thereafter adopted a demonic gimmick in Florida. He's the brainchild of gimmicks like the Dungeon of Doom and has been the matchmaker in Florida, WCW, and Smoky Mountain. Has also managed a bevy of sordid characters over the years. [Dungeon Master; Task Master]

Sullivan, Nancy
(1980s-2000s)

Nancy broke into wrestling as a valet for Ron Simmons and Butch Reed in WCW and was often aligned with the occult. With an Elvira-like demeanor and a model's looks, she was very successful on air. [Robin Green; Woman]

Sytch, Tammy
(1990s-2000s)

One of the prettiest women to circle ringside, she began as a television announcer in Smoky Mountain Wrestling in 1992, but quickly ascended the ladder to the WWF in 1995 where she managed her boyfriend Chris Candido and Tom Pritchard (as the Body Donnas). More than any female before her, she showed Vince McMahon Jr. how valuable sex appeal could be in wrestling. Her success led to personalities like Sable and Torrie Wilson. [Sunny]

Tajiri
(1990s-2000s)

He was just one of the pack in Japan, so native Yoshihiro Tajiri came to the U.S. in the late 1990s via ECW. It proved to be a smart move. Perhaps no other Japanese has had as much American success in the early century as this buzz saw. He brought several innovative moves with him and used them to win the ECW tag-team title with Mikey Whipwreck. Once in the WWF, he has been a solid addition to the cruiserweight division, winning the belt in 2001. [Yoshihiro Tajiri]

Takada, Nobuhiko
(1980s-2000s)

A widely recognized
shooter from Japan, the
tall star was a middle of
the pack heavyweight
and tag-team partner
of Akira Maeda in New
Japan when he broke
off with the renegade
Maeda to form the shoot-
fighting group, UWF. He
saw great success there,
but eventually went back
to his roots in 1996 in
winning the pro wrestling
IWGP championship from
Keiji Mutoh. He's also
appeared in Pride Fighting
Championships.

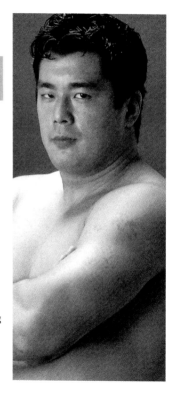

Tanaka, Masato
(1990s-2000s)

With a forehead of steel, Tanaka made a name for himself in Japan as part of the hardcore group, FMW. Known to take multiple blows to the head, he always gets back up. He's a short, stocky, fireplug.

Tanaka, Toru
(1960s-1980s)

One of the most powerful Asian grapplers, he won numerous U.S. tag-team titles in the 1970s. The barefooted wrestler settled in Los Angeles and wrestled into the 1980s. In addition to wrestling, he was a veteran of many feature films, including "The Running Man." [Prof. Tanaka]

Tarzan Goto
(1980s-2000s)

Few wrestlers sport as many scars on their body as Tarzan, an insane hardcore wrestler from Japan. Legs, arms, you name it—Goto's got them scarred. His career began in the U.S. Central States area, where he trained with Mr. Pogo. He feuded with Onita through much of the 1990s and bounced around to virtually every hardcore territory in Japan. He and Onita wrestled in the first barbed wire explosion match on FMW's debut card in 1990. Later, he trained Hayabusa. In the early 2000s, he was still carving his body.

Taylor, Chris
(1970s)

One of the first wrestlers to sign a guaranteed contract, Taylor, a collegiate wrestler from Iowa State, was nabbed by Verne Gagne for $100,000 to be the next baby-faced superstar. At 400-plus pounds, he was the biggest Olympic wrestler on record when he won the Bronze freestyle medal in 1972. Tons of promise, his size eventually caught up with him. After time in the AWA, he died in 1979 at the age of 29.

Former Olympic medalist Chris Taylor splashes a hapless foe.

Taylor, Scott
(1990s-2000s)

This light heavyweight reminds fans of Eddie Gilbert and Buck Zumhoff. It's hard for any small wrestler to get a break, so Taylor needed to invent some fun. As Scotty Too Hotty in the WWF, he formed a tag-team with Brian Lawler and Rikishi called Too Cool and won the tag-team championship. As a singles wrestler, he won the company's lightweight title from Dean Malenko in 2000. [Scotty Too Hotty]

Taylor, Terry
(1980s-2000s)

Should Taylor have been an NWA champion? Some think so. But just as his career was on the rise, this tactician inherited the worst gimmick of all time—the Red Rooster—and it ruined his career. In Mid-South, Taylor lit up crowds in performances against Chris Adams, Eddie Gilbert, Steve Williams, and Ted DiBiase. Despite his size, he seemed destined for greatness. He took the money in the WWF and he never recovered. A former UWF TV champion, he split from the WWF and returned to WCW to try and recapture what was lost. Since then, Taylor has been a road agent for all major groups. [Red Rooster; Terrence Taylor]

Tazz
(1990s-2000s)

Too short, too dull, too quiet to make it. Those were the knocks on Tazz before he was unleashed by Paul Heyman in ECW. For several years, he toiled in the independents because of size, but Heyman saw something more. He underwent a personality transplant and became the street thug, Tazz. With carefully crafted interviews, he caught fire and won two ECW world titles and two tag-team titles. Before ECW folded, he bolted for the WWF and began another career as a television broadcaster. [Tasmaniac; Taz]

Tenyru, Genichiro
(1970s-2000s)

The Great Tenyru has earned his rep as a Japanese hero. He's been a promoter and booker and has headlined singles and tag-team matches. Although he seemed to play second fiddle in Japan with Baba and Inoki roaming in the 1980s, he was always at the top of every group he wrestled in. He's held the prestigious All-Japan Triple Crown title two times, beating Jumbo Tsuruta and Toshiaki Kawada. In 1999, he beat Keiji Mutoh to win the IWGP Grand Prix belt. [Great Tenyru]

Thatcher, Les
(1960s-2000s)

In his day, Thatcher
was a top Mid-Atlantic
junior heavyweight.
Since retirement, he's
been an announcer for
many promotions in the
Southeast. Since the early
1990s, he's owned and
operated the Heartland
Wrestling Association in
Ohio, which for a time,
was a WWE training
facility.

Thesz, Lou
(1940s-1990s)

Is he the best of all time? That's often a topic of great debate, but no one questions the legacy and importance of Thesz, a six-time NWA world champion. Born of Hungarian ancestry, he turned pro in the 1930s and won his first title at age 21 by defeating Everett Marshall. Equally as impressive, his sixth belt was won in 1963 at age 46. His list of past challengers are literally a "who's who" of wrestling legends. He was revered in Japan, which oddly enough, supported him more than Americans. A conditioning freak, he wrestled his last match in his 70s. Born Lajos Tiza, he died in 2002 at age 86.

Tiger Mask
(1980s-2000s)

This oft-used wrestling gimmick, based after a children's cartoon, has become legendary in Japan. Satoru Sayama, the first to use the mask, turned pro in 1980 and amazed crowds with his revolutionary dives and cat-like reflexes. On one of his first U.S. tours, he won the NWA and WWF junior heavyweight belts on consecutive nights. His legendary matches with Dynamite Kid, Black Tiger, and Davey Boy Smith are classics and inspired people like Jerry Lynn, Chris Benoit, and the late Owen Hart. The Japanese star truly revolutionized the industry and today's business owes him a debt of thanks.

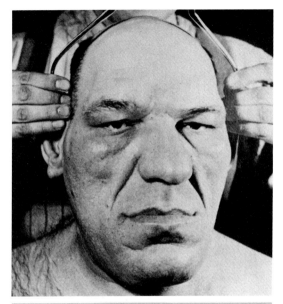

Tillet, Maurice
(1920s-1940s)

The original French Angel, he was a human oddity. Weighing more than 300 pounds with an enormous head and set of hands, he held one version of the world title. He died in 1951 at age 54.

Tolos, John
(1950s-1990s)

The "Golden Greek"
was an accomplished star
and the ideal traveling
heel who would invade a
new territory, create a stir
by wrestling the top hero,
and then leave for another
territory. He often used the
stomach claw as a finisher.
During the 1960s, he was
noted for his bloodbath
feuds with Fred Blassie
and the Destroyer. In the
early 1990s, long after
retirement, he managed
Curt Hennig briefly in
the WWF. [Coach; Golden
Greek]

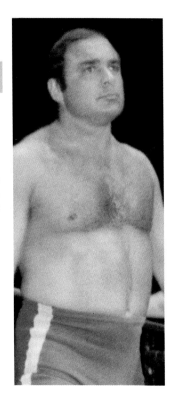

Tori
(1980s-2000s)

Known for her bodybuilding prowess, this former women's wrestler-turned-valet wrestled from Japan to the Northwest, LPWA, and WWF. She held regional women's belts, but departed wrestling altogether. [Terri Powers]

Triple H
(1990s-2000s)

Triple H's rise through the ranks has been impressive. Originally a bodybuilder, he looked to Killer Kowalski for wrestling training. After a failed start in WCW, he's consistently improved since his WWE debut in 1995. Known as a backroom politico, he's gone from the goofy character Hunter Hearst Helmsley to the modern HHH, a six-time world champion. He was a member of the group Degeneration X, which helped the WWE regain its fan base in the late 1990s. In WWE, he's held every major belt and has been ingrained in main events since 1999. [The Game; Hunter Hearst Helmsley; Jean Paul Levesque; Terra Ryzin]

Tsuruta, Jumbo
(1970s-1990s)

One of Japan's most revered wrestlers until his death in 1999. He was an Olympic wrestler in 1972 and based on his fame, Giant Baba signed him to an All-Japan deal. During the 1980s and 1990s, few wrestlers were as big as Tsuruta. In the U.S., he trained with the Funk family. His main-event status was highlighted with three runs as the Triple Crown champion and multiple runs as tag-team champ. His success also followed him to the United States. In 1984, he defeated Nick Bockwinkel for the AWA world title. While the names Baba and Inoki loom large in Japan, the name Jumbo lies not far behind.

Ultimate Warrior, The
(1980s-1990s)

Jim Hellwig started his career as Sting's partner in a Mid-South team called the Blade Runners. The two were discovered during their involvement in the California-based Power Team USA bodybuilding squad. Hellwig took off for World Class where he won the Texas title as the Dingo Warrior. The WWF came calling and he became the Ultimate Warrior, winning the Intercontinental and world titles, the latter by beating Hulk Hogan at Wrestlemania 7. But turmoil followed. Hellwig left wrestling and sued the WWF to use his ring name. In the end, he was able to call himself The Warrior. [Dingo Warrior; Warrior]

Undertaker, The
(1980s-2000s)

Born from the mold of tough Texans such as the Funk and Rhodes families, Mark Calloway bided his time before finding the right gimmick at the right time. He toiled in USWA and WCW with nondescript personalities when, in 1990, he was brought to the WWF to work with the Undertaker gimmick. Rather than balk at the gimmickry, he brought life to the character, which has been one of the most successful concoctions in WWE history. Despite constant injuries, he's held the world title three times since his debut. [American Badass; Master of Pain; Mean Mark; Punisher]

Vachon, Luna
(1980s-2000s)

Not only does she look the part, she's lived a life on the edge. Luna, short for Lunatic, has played a post-apocalyptic wrestler with face paint and a wild demeanor. This female member of the Vachon family began wrestling in the late 1980s as part of the GLOW group, but kept her career moving and eventually made it to the WWF.

Vachon, Maurice
(1940s-1980s)

An Olympic wrestler from the 1948 Canadian National team, Vachon struggled to crossover to the pros until he met up with Portland promoter Don Owen who dubbed Vachon the "Mad Dog." From there, Vachon became a legendary wrestler and brawler who employed an aggressive, no-nonsense style. He was a main event star from the 1940s to 1980s and knew two styles in the ring: fast and faster. Along with his brother, Paul Vachon, they won many tag-team titles. Mad Dog even won the AWA world title twice in the 1960s. [Mad Dog Vachon]

Vachon, Paul
(1960s-1980s)

Although he was larger than his brother, Maurice, Paul Vachon's career was not quite as hot. Even so, he was a reliable, solid competitor who performed in the AWA, WWF, WWA, and Canada. He shaved his head and wrestled with a full beard, a distinct look indeed. His feuds against Harley Race, Larry Hennig, the Crusher, and Bruiser drew large crowds in the AWA. [Butcher Vachon]

Vachon, Vivian
(1970s-1980s)

The daughter of Paul Vachon, Viv was one of the most revered and respected women wrestlers of her day. In addition to her ring work, she was a popular French-Canadian vocalist. Sadly, she died from injuries suffered in a car accident in 1991.

Vader
(1980s-2000s)

Leon White began as an AWA mid-card wrestler in the 1980s, but there was little demand for a 30-ish, balding, ex-football player—that was, until he fell into the Big Van Vader gimmick. Reportedly, New Japan and Disney trademarked the name and a signature mask worn by White that blew smoke as he entered the arena. It was quite a spectacle. The smoke left Japanese crowds going nuts. He's known as the only wrestler to hold world titles from four countries simultaneously: Mexico, Germany, U.S., and Japan. Equal to his gimmick was his ability in the ring. Though he was more than 300 pounds, he could do moonsaults and brawl with the best. Among his accolades: two-time Triple Crown champion, three-time IWGP champion, and three-time WCW world champion. [Big Van Vader; Leon White]

Valentine, Greg
(1970s-2000s)

The legit son of 1960s star Johnny Valentine, he originally wrestled as Johnny Fargo so not to be lost in his dad's footsteps. He eventually became a world star as Valentine. He toured the NWA and WWF feuding with and against Roddy Piper. The beefy Valentine was a former Intercontinental champion and tag-team titleholder with Brutus Beefcake. [Blue Knight; Johnny Fargo]

Valentine, Johnny
(1960s-1970s)

Valentine was known for being a rough ring bully and backstage prankster—often going over the line. He was sometimes alienated by his peers, but he was always in high demand with promoters. The father of Greg Valentine could make an entire arena erupt on the drop of a dime. He toured Mid-Atlantic extensively, winning many titles there, until his early retirement in 1975 from injures suffered in a plane crash. He died in 2001.

Valiant, Jimmy
(1970s-1990s)

This talented and blond rock 'n' roll wrestler was an ideal tag-team wrestler. He had a swagger, adequate skills, and later, was a great interview. Since the mid-1980s, he teamed with "brothers" Johnny and Jerry in the WWWF. In 1974, Jimmy and Johnny were crowned world tag-team champions. As a single's star, he won the Memphis Southern title four times in the late 1970s. [Charlie Brown]

Valiant, Johnny
(1960s-1990s)

The 1970s were a powerful time for tag teams and Johnny, along with Jimmy Valiant, made up one of the most colorful. His real name is Johnny Sullivan and he was a ring veteran who took on numerous names and identities. With his skills waning, he took on Jimmy as his partner and together they were magical. They won the WWWF tag-team titles in 1974 in a win over Tony Garea and Dean Ho. When his wrestling career ended, Valiant went on to managing in the WWF, leading such stars as Greg Valentine, Brutus Beefcake, and Bob Orton Jr.

Johnny Valient took control when he entered the ring.

Vampiro
(1980s-2000s)

Once homeless in Los Angeles, he had designs on a music career when, virtually on a whim, he took off for Mexico. With limited ring experience under his belt, Vampiro hooked up with the EMLL promotion in Mexico City. He was an immediate hit, performing to sold-out crowds with his unique style and misfit appearance. He rode the success to the UWA world title in 1992, and later the WCW tag titles with the Great Muta. [Canadian Vampire]

Van Dam, Rob
(1980s-2000s)

You can't say Van Dam hasn't marched to his own beat. The Michigan native didn't look to have a future in wrestling as a television jobber for WCW in the late 1980s. His Jean Claude Van Dam appearance and martial arts flexibility weren't enough to bring him success. But when he was approached by ECW, everything changed and he was allowed to be himself. His following gave the fledgling promotion life. He had classic matches with Sabu, the Public Enemy, and Jerry Lynn, winning the TV and tag-team titles. Since then, he's become an integral part of the WWE family.

Van Hammer
(1980s-1990s)

With WCW searching for new talent in the late 1980s, the company brought in Hammer. He had a good look (think cross between Sammy Hagar and Lex Luger), but he was never able to put the whole package together. He returned to WCW in the late 1990s, but later disappeared. [Hammer]

Ventura, Jesse
(1970s-2000s)

Jesse has really done it all. He's been in the military, he's been to Wrestlemania, and he's had face-to-face meetings with Cuban dictator Fidel Castro. His election as Minnesota governor in 1998 is his crowning achievement. After debuting in 1979 in the mold of his favorite wrestler, Billy Graham, Ventura's personality-plus gimmick helped solidify him as a great entertainer. As a wrestler, he left something to be desired. After runs in the Northwest and AWA, he bolted for the WWF in 1983. An illness in 1984 ended his wrestling career, but he rejuvenated himself as an announcer and actor. [Surfer Jesse]

Jesse Ventura was not afraid to show his strength.

Vicious, Sid
(1980s-2000s)

This monster has been to the mountain and back again. Seen in VFWs in front of 10 people, he's also headlined Wrestlemania. At 6'7", he looked like a promoter's dream. He began his career in the Continental area, and then took off for WCW, where he teamed with Dan Spivey. Eventually he made his way to WWF, where he was a two-time world champion; he also won the WCW world title twice. A major knee injury ended his career in 2000. [Lord Humongous; Psycho Sid; Sid Justice]

Sid Vicious didn't mince words.

Victoria
(2000s)

This vibrant brunette is a former fitness model who was discovered in Southern California. Part crazy but all beauty, she's been a WWE women's champ with feuds against Trish Stratus and Jackie.

Victory, Jack
(1980s-2000s)

A man of a million gimmicks, the pudgy Victory has been to almost every territory, in roles like a secret serviceman, bodyguard, and militiaman. He's a very complementary wrestler to several tag partners, but he was best as Jack Victory in which he held the UWF tag title in 1986 with longtime partner John Tatum.

Von Erich, Chris
(1980s)

The smallest and youngest of the Von Erich family, Chris, at 5'4", seemed to be jinxed from the get-go. He tried to follow his successful brothers into the wrestling business by wrestling for World Class in its waning days, but he couldn't rally beyond his height. Sadly, he committed suicide in 1991 at age 21.

Von Erich, David
(1970s-1980s)

Each Von Erich family member had something to offer and David was no exception. Considered the best wrestler in the family, the tall and popular commodity was hot not only in Dallas, but in Japan as brother Kevin's tag-team partner. In his home state, he was a four-time Texas champion. He appeared poised for an NWA title reign when he died suddenly in 1984 while on tour in Japan from an intestinal disorder, although drug use was suspected. He was 25.

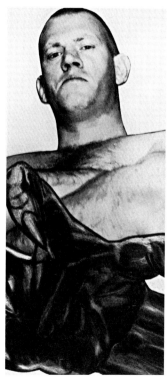

Von Erich, Fritz
(1950s-1990s)

Fritz Adkisson had a big, menacing ring style using a German gimmick. He held numerous belts with his "brother" Waldo and he held the World Class American title 11 times from 1966-82. The master of the iron claw, Fritz turned his success into a powerful family business in Dallas. All five of his children became wrestlers and sadly, four died in their primes. But in his family's heyday—the late 1970s and early 1980s—their company in Dallas was the hottest wrestling territory in the country. Fritz passed away in 1997.

Von Erich, Kerry
(1980s-1990s)

Kerry was the most recognized name in the Von Erich family. In 1984, Kerry won the NWA world title from Ric Flair. After a dynamic career in Dallas, where he won the WCCW world title three times, Kerry took off for the WWF, where he won the Intercontinental title in 1990 from another second-generation star, Curt Hennig. Unbeknownst to people around him, Kerry had a portion of his foot amputated after a motorcycle crash, yet he continued to wrestle valiantly with a prosthesis. He was cursed by inner demons and drug use from chronic pain. He committed suicide in 1993 at age 33. [Texas Tornado]

Von Erich, Kevin
(1970s-1990s)

The only Von Erich son still alive, Kevin was a four-time Texas champion and five-time American champion. Through the early 1980s, like the entire Von Erich family, he was consumed by his family's feud with the Freebirds. Often, Kevin shared the ring with his brothers in six-man tag matches against the "Birds." After Kerry's death in 1993, Kevin wrestled briefly but retired in 1995. Today, he has tried to move on from the pain his family endured and is settled in with his family on their Texas ranch.

Von Erich, Mike
(1980s)

No one would have envied Mike's position following his brother David's death in 1984. He was thrust into Dave's spot, but Mike, at age 20, clearly wasn't ready. In six-man competition, he faired well helping his brothers win the world titles four times. He also had a run as the American champ. While on tour in Japan, he contracted toxic shock syndrome, an illness he barely recovered from. Unable to perform to his own standards, he took his own life in 1987 at age 23.

Von Raschke, Baron
(1960s-1990s)

Jim Raschke was an all-star who wrestled and played football at Nebraska when Verne Gagne discovered him. Using his real name, he failed to catch on. Like many in his day, he became a goose-stepping German in the ring. That was smart, as he became a singles star throughout the U.S. He toured the world using his gimmick, but eventually settled right where he had begun—in the Midwest.

Watson, Billy
(1940s-1960s)

Toronto-based main-event star who was a former two-time world champion. Despite his Canadian appeal, he found success in the U.S. After a series of matches against Lou Thesz for the Canadian title, Watson was deemed the No. 1 challenger to the NWA world title. In 1947, he beat Bill Longson for his first title. He later beat Thesz for the world belt in 1956. [Whipper Watson]

Watts, Bill
(1950s-1990s)

This rough cowboy from Oklahoma was a major player as a wrestler and promoter. He had a short-lived pro football career with the Houston Oilers in 1961. After being welcomed to wrestling by Leroy McGuirk and Danny Hodge, his biggest days in the ring were in the 1960s. Popularly used around the Midwest and Mid-South, he was a five-time North American champion. By the time he retired, his new career began. He promoted the Mid-South/UWF region, using top caliber stars like Ted DiBiase and Steve Williams, up until he sold the territory in 1986 to Jim Crockett Jr. He was briefly the matchmaker for WCW in the early 1990s, but by then, his style wasn't considered current enough to be profitable.

Wayne, Ken
(1980s-1990s)

Diminutive but talented, "The Nightmare" was a frequent partner of Danny Davis in several tag teams. Across the Southeast, Wayne performed under tag-team names like the Nightmares, Galaxians, and Masters of Terror.

Whatley, Pez
(1970s-1980s)

Wearing a top hat and tails, this smiling man was a popularly used attraction in Texas and in Mid-South. Mainly a heel in his career, the onetime Florida Southern champion was a tag-team partner of the large Ray Candy and second-generation star, Tiger Conway Jr (as the Jive Tones). Passed away in 2005. [Shaska Whatley]

Wild Samoans, The
(1960s-1980s)

Afa and Sika were a wildly successful oddity team and are actually brothers. They ruled the East Coast and were hardcore before hardcore was cool. In addition to winning the WWF tag titles three times from 1980-83, they toured Japan, Puerto Rico, and Canada. They've left a tremendous legacy as nearly a dozen relatives and family members have broken into wrestling including Rikishi, Tonga Kid, Three Minute Warning, the Rock, and the late Yokozuna. Now retired, they operate an independent group out of Pennsylvania.

Williams, Steve
(1980s-2000s)

A native of Oklahoma, he was a natural in Mid-South. After wrestling and playing football for the Sooners—he was a three-time Big 12 conference wrestling champion—and in the defunct USFL pro-league, he debuted for Watts in 1982. He was a mean-looking bruiser and brawler. He won several titles for Watts. After a stint in the NWA, winning the world tag titles with Mike Rotunda, he headed for a prolific career in Japan in the mold of Bruiser Brody. In the 1990s, he and Terry Gordy were arguably the top Americans there. Likely, there won't be another like Williams again. [Dr. Death]

Wilson, Torrie
(1990s-2000s)

Fitness modeling just wasn't enough for the Idaho native. Lured to wrestling by WCW, she's been a valet, manager, and wrestler in WWE. Her popularity and appeal led to lots of face time on TV. [Miss NWO; Samantha]

Windham, Barry
(1970s-2000s)

This second-generation wrestler has had several gimmicks, but always did best as Barry. He's led a career full of highlights despite some dull years. In 1993, the son of Blackjack Mulligan won the NWA world title from the Great Muta. In his youth, he had the grace of a true technician despite his 6'7, 240-pound frame. In the WWF, he won the world tag title with Mike Rotunda, before heading back to WCW. He won the Florida title four times and his series with Ric Flair during that period was phenomenal and have people remembering him as a modern-day great. [Blackjack Jr.; Stalker; Widowmaker]

Windham, Kendall
(1980s-1990s)

The less-accomplished son of Blackjack Mulligan, he was a beanpole when he started in Florida in the early 1980s. Even so, he trudged on and had minor success in that state and in the NWA, where he sometimes teamed with brother, Barry.

Wright, Alex
(1990s-2000s)

This German phenom could use the ropes with the best of them. In WCW, he was a cruiserweight, television, and tag-team champion, and popular attraction at that. [Berlyn]

X-Pac
(1980s-2000s)

Sean Waltman began his career at age 15 at the Malenko school in Florida before moving to Minnesota. There, he combined styles from Japan, Calgary, and Mexico. Has he always been in the right place at the right time? That's what put him in the middle of two revolutionary angles, the New World Order and Degeneration X. Among his titles: one WCW cruiserweight title, two WWF lightweight titles, and four WWF tag-team titles. [1-2-3 Kid; Kid; Lightning Kid; Syxx; Syxx-Pac]

Yokozuna
(1980s-1990s)

Rodney Anoia, a revered member of the Samoan wrestling clan, lived large. His uncles were the great Afa and Sika. A two-time WWF champion and tag-team champion with the late Owen Hart, he wrestled in the AWA, Mexico, and Japan before hitting the WWF in 1992. His size—at one point he weighed more than 600 pounds—was his livelihood, but it also caused his early death. He was once named Kokina Maximus as a joke, which referred to his large backside. Despite efforts to lose weight, he died in 2000 from heart failure at age 34. [Great Kokina; Kokina Maximus]

Young, Mae
(1930s-2000s)

Although she never won the world title herself, Young is an amazing eight-decade performer. A good friend of Fabulous Moolah, she even turned up in the WWF since 1999 and has provided many laughs.

Youngbloods, The
(1980s-1990s)

Mark and Chris Romero were second-generation talents who fought to catch on outside the Kansas-Missouri region. With an eye to the future, they adopted the Youngblood name and with it, became known in many promotions. Although very small, they wrestled out of the Mid-Atlantic and Texas promotions using a Native American gimmick to minimal success. Later on, they found success in Puerto Rico and Japan.

Zbyszko, Larry
(1970s-2000s)

As Larry Whistler, few fans appreciated him until he was "adopted" by Bruno Sammartino in WWF storylines. Eventually, he feuded with his mentor Bruno and the two met at Shea Stadium in 1980. From that feud, he called himself the "Living Legend." Known for his fine interview skills, he was a multi-promotion champion and the last to hold the AWA world title in 1990.

Zeus
(1980s-2000s)

He had a short career but it's hard to forget him. The scary looking Tiny Lister is from Orange County, California. After the film was released, Zeus took off around the horn and headlined several shows with Ted DiBiase against Hogan. Since then, he's been in dozens of B-grade action flicks.

Zumhoff, Buck
(1970s-2000s)

This four-decade light heavyweight worked his way from ring crew to referee to titleholder in the AWA. Known as the "Rock & Roller," he carried a boom box to the ring in his heyday and rode that gimmick to success in the Midwest and Texas.

Index

C

D

E